PIRATES · EXPLORERS
TRAILBLAZERS

WRITTEN BY PAMELA AMICK KLAWITTER
ILLUSTRATED BY BEVERLY ARMSTRONG

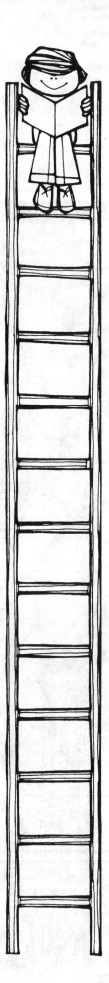

The Learning Works

Edited by Sherri M. Butterfield

Contents

Contents
(continued)

To the Teacher

The activities in this book have been selected especially for gifted students in grades 4 through 6 and are designed to challenge them and to help them develop and apply higher-level thinking skills. These activities have been grouped by subject matter into the following three sections: Pirates, Explorers, and Trailblazers.

Pirates

Pirates have haunted the world's waterways since the days of the first Phoenician traders. During the seventeenth and eighteenth centuries, these buccaneers plundered shipping in such numbers that the economies of some countries were threatened. Historians call this period the "golden age of piracy." It is primarily with the seafarers of this period that this unit deals.

A colorful era, to be sure, this period spawned its share of legendary characters. Examined here are some of the real-life treasure-seekers who plagued the sea-lanes, as well as some of the legends that have grown up around their misdeeds. Also discussed are ships and other tools of the trade.

Explorers

The unknown has lured man since the beginning of time. Prehistoric hunters searching for food were probably the first explorers, but this unit deals with the golden age of exploration, when kings and queens sent explorers into the unknown to seek riches and lands for settlement.

The activities in this unit are designed to (1) acquaint students with some of the major European explorers who sought trade routes to the Far East, (2) develop an awareness of the problems faced by those who ventured into new worlds, and (3) build an appreciation of the courage and spirit that these adventurers shared.

Trailblazers

A special breed of explorer is examined in this unit. Some of the men and women who opened up the continental United States to settlement are introduced. The stages of westward expansion are also discussed.

In this unit, students will read about the various groups who were instrumental in leading the way west—such as frontiersmen, trappers, explorers, soldiers, missionaries, and gold seekers—and about some of the outstanding individuals who contributed to this country's growth. Activities are designed to develop an understanding of the many obstacles that stood in the way of westward movement and an appreciation of the ingenious ways in which these obstacles were overcome.

To the Teacher
(continued)

Within each of these three sections are bulletin board ideas, learning center ideas, a pretest and a posttest, as many as twenty-one activity pages, an answer page, and an award to be given to students who satisfactorily complete the unit of study. These materials may be used with your entire class, for small-group instruction, or by individual students working independently at their desks or at learning centers. Although you may want to elaborate on the information presented, each activity has been described so that students can do it without additional instruction.

All of the activities in this book are designed to provide experiences and instruction that are qualitatively different and to promote development and use of higher-level thinking skills. For your convenience, they have been coded according to Bloom's taxonomy. The symbols used in this coding process are as follows:

KN **knowledge** recall of specific bits of information; the student absorbs, remembers, recognizes, and responds.

CO **comprehension** understanding of communicated material without relating it to other material; the student explains, translates, demonstrates, and interprets.

AP **application** using methods, concepts, principles, and theories in new situations; the student solves novel problems, demonstrates use of knowledge, and constructs.

AN **analysis** breaking down a communication into its constituent elements; the student discusses, uncovers, lists, and dissects.

SY **synthesis** putting together constituent elements or parts to form a whole; the student discusses, generalizes, relates, compares, contrasts, and abstracts.

EV **evaluation** judging the value of materials and methods given purposes; applying standards and criteria, the student judges and disputes.

These symbols have been placed in the left-hand margin beside the corresponding activity description. Usually, you will find only one symbol; however, some activities involve more than one level of thinking or consist of several parts, each involving a different level. In these instances, several symbols have been used.

KN CO AP AN SY EV

Pirates

Bulletin Board Ideas

Treasury of Pirate Facts

1. Draw and cut out letters to spell the words **Treasury of Pirate Facts.**
2. Draw and cut out a pirate trunk or treasure chest.
3. Post the letters and the chest on a bulletin board.
4. From gold or yellow paper and from silver or gray paper, cut circles to resemble coins.
5. Post these coins on the bulletin board or make them available in a container nearby.
6. Encourage students to write facts about pirates on the coins in the form of a question on one side and the answer on the other side.
7. Use these coins to MC "question bees" or quiz shows about pirates or to find the treasure "buried" below.

Buried Treasure

1. Create a simple map on which a segmented path leads from the water's edge past several hazards and distinctive features to the site of buried treasure.
2. Divide the class into teams.
3. Give each team a different paper pirate flag to be used as a marker.
4. Allow team members to carry their flags forward toward the site of the treasure each time they add a question about pirates to the treasury or each time they answer a question about pirates correctly.
5. The first team to reach the buried treasure wins.

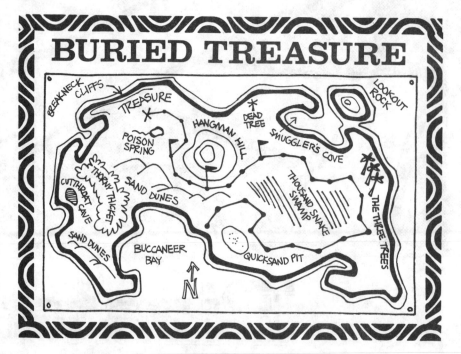

Learning Center Idea

Design a flag for a pirate vessel.

Pirate ships were powered by the wind in their sails. Discover what these sails were made of and where this material came from. Compare this material with that used for sails today. Which one is heavier? Which one is stronger? Why?

Meals aboard a pirate ship were nothing like those served on a cruise ship today. First, do some research to learn what pirates ate. Then, create a menu for a typical evening meal aboard a pirate ship.

Pirate Projects

Look up these names for pirates and learn how their etymologies and meanings differ.

brigand   privateer
buccaneer   rogue
corsair   swashbuckler
freebooter   sea dog
picaroon   sea rover

Add these words to your maritime vocabulary.

aft   fore
boom   jib
bow   mast
bowsprit   port
bumpkin   starboard
crow's nest   stern
        sterncastle

Write job descriptions for these members of a pirate crew.
captain
quartermaster
lieutenant
sailing master
boatswain

Pirates and others who sailed the seas used ships with these names.

biremes   galleons
brigantines   galleys
caravels   schooners
carracks   sloops
flutes   snows

In what ways are these ships similar?
In what ways are they different?

Name _____

Pretest

Circle the letter beside the best answer or the most appropriate response.

1. "Blackbeard" was the nickname given to
   a. Stede Bonnet.
   b. Edward Teach.
   c. Sir Henry Morgan.
   d. William Kidd.

2. Which one of these pirates lived long enough to enjoy the "fruits" of his labor?
   a. Black Bart
   b. Sir Henry Morgan
   c. Calico Jack
   d. Edward England

3. **Salmagundi** was
   a. a disease that often afflicted pirates on long voyages.
   b. an exotic stew.
   c. an island off the coast of Africa.
   d. a tribal chief on Madagascar.

4. Pirates of the Barbary Coast were known as
   a. buccaneers.
   b. filibusters.
   c. picaroons.
   d. corsairs.

5. Which one of these words is *not* the name of a type of ship?
   a. flute
   b. brigand
   c. snow
   d. brigantine

6. Which one of these words is *not* a nickname for a pirate?
   a. bandolier
   b. swashbuckler
   c. picaroon
   d. cutthroat

7. The group named by this word originally performed a legalized type of piracy.
   a. picaroons
   b. freebooters
   c. brigands
   d. privateers

8. The **sailing master's** main job was to
   a. take over in event of the captain's death.
   b. mete out punishment for petty crimes.
   c. divide the plunder.
   d. set the sails and steer the ship.

9. The **boatswain**
   a. cared for the ship's tackle and supplies.
   b. took charge of the ship's weaponry.
   c. administered floggings.
   d. was first to board a "prize" after battle.

10. Which one of these terms names a punishment that probably was not widely administered by pirates?
    a. flogging
    b. marooning
    c. walking the plank
    d. Moses' Law

Name _____

The Golden Age of Piracy

Piracy, as robbery on the high seas is called, is now against the law of every nation; but it was not always so. In ancient times, the Minoans of Crete became the undisputed rulers of the seas only after they put professional soldiers aboard each sailing vessel to protect its cargo and crew against pirates. Phoenicians, Greeks, and Romans risked having their cargoes stolen anytime they sailed on the Aegean or Mediterranean Sea. During the seventeenth and eighteenth centuries, piracy was a commonly accepted hazard of sea travel. And as recently as the nineteenth century, merchant vessels were often at the mercy of pirates, who captured crews and stole cargoes of gold, silver, silks, spices, and anything else of value.

The seventeenth and early eighteenth centuries are known as the "golden age of piracy." During this period, pirates became so powerful that they even established their own coastal encampments from which they could watch shipping lanes and attack merchant vessels sailing the coasts of North and South America and of Africa. Madagascar and the Bahamas became cutthroats' lairs. The irregular coastlines of these islands and of the **Spanish Main**—as the northern coast of the South American mainland was called—provided an endless array of coves and inlets in which pirate ships could easily be sheltered and concealed. From their hiding places, these ships would sail out to attack Spanish galleons carrying New World riches to Old World ports.

It was during this golden age that pirates like Black Bart, Blackbeard, Captain Kidd, and Calico Jack roamed the seas in search of booty and lived the lives that made them legends.

Activities

KN CO 1. Find out what type of ships the Phoenicians used to carry on their trade. On a separate sheet of paper, sketch one of these ships and list the cargo that might have been found aboard.

KN CO AP 2. Coins were the most sought-after booty for pirate crews because they could be quickly and evenly divided among greedy thieves. Make a large chart. Divide the chart into three columns. Label these columns **Name of Coin**, **Sketch of Coin**, and **Country of Origin**. Down the left-hand side of the chart, under the column heading **Name of Coin**, list the following ten coins: **crown, crusado, denier, doubloon, ducat, guinea, louis d'or, mohur, piece of eight**, and **shilling**. Do whatever research is necessary to make appropriate entries in the other two columns.

KN CO AP 3. Many authors have written true or fictionalized accounts of treasure hunts and pirate escapades. First, write the names of these three authors down the left-hand side of a piece of paper: Sir James Barrie, Rafael Sabatini, and Robert Louis Stevenson. Next, look up each one in an encyclopedia or biographical dictionary to discover what stories or books he wrote. Then, write the titles of their pirate-related works beside their names. Finally, choose one of these works, read it, and report on it to other members of the class.

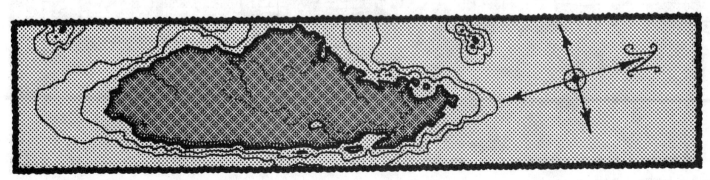

The History of Piracy

Because the pirates we read about in books or see in movies typify those of the seventeenth and eighteenth centuries, we are inclined to think that robbery on the high seas took place only during this period. In reality, piracy was a profitable business as many as three thousand years ago. The ships of Phoenicia, the greatest seafaring nation of the ancient world, were harassed by pirates. The Minoans assigned professional soldiers to protect the cargoes and crews of their sailing vessels as they plied the waters of the Aegean, Ionian, and Mediterranean seas. The early Greeks practiced piracy and delighted in displaying their booty in the marketplace after a successful raid.

In Roman times, bands of pirates built fortified cities along the Aegean and Mediterranean coasts. One such band even captured the young Julius Caesar during the first century B.C. and held him for ransom. Caesar later became a Roman general. In this capacity, he extended the power of the Roman Empire throughout most of the known world. While the empire was strong, its rulers controlled piracy by means of well-trained patrol fleets. For more than two hundred and fifty years, the seas of the Mediterranean world were a relatively safe place on which to travel. But when the empire weakened, pirates once again took control of the shipping lanes.

During the Middle Ages, pirates from the Barbary Coast of Northern Africa wreaked havoc on Mediterranean shipping. These Muslim pirates, known as **corsairs**, raided European coastal cities and captured Christians, whom they took back to Africa to be sold as slaves. As recently as 1801, these pirates still posed such a threat to American shipping that President Thomas Jefferson sent armed ships to protect American merchant vessels sailing in this area.

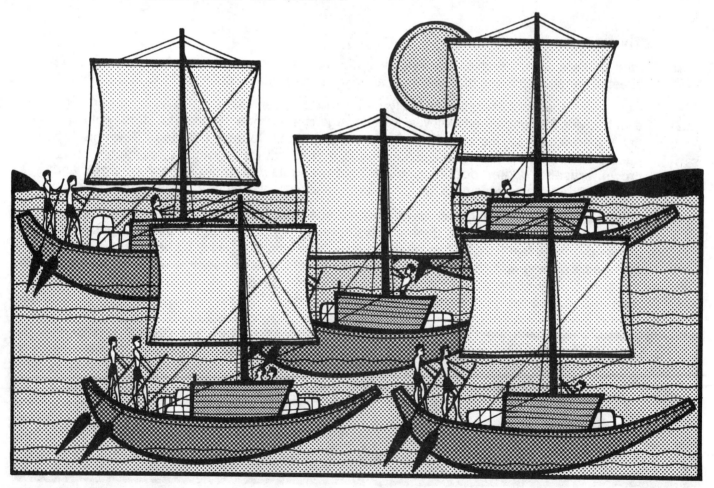

Name _____

The History of Piracy
(continued)

Most pirates were independent agents. They were neither restricted nor protected by any nation or government. And they owed neither allegiance nor commission to any ruler. Instead, they roamed the coasts and seas attacking the unprotected ships of any nation.

Privateers were different. They were the commanders and crew members of armed, privately owned vessels hired by the ruler of one nation for the purpose of attacking the ships of an enemy nation.

During the sixteenth and seventeenth centuries, Spanish ships laden with New World gold and other riches sailed regularly from the Spanish Main back to their home ports. Because Queen Elizabeth I wanted England to have a share of this treasure, she authorized raids by buccaneers along the Caribbean coast of South America and hired privateers to attack Spanish ships. Together, these pirate groups were so successful that they hastened Spain's decline as a world power.

Activities

KN
CO
1. Ancient Roman sailors and their more modern Spanish counterparts are not the only people who were repeatedly plagued by pirates. Do some research to learn about Viking raids along the northern European and English coasts or about Japanese raids against China. Share what you learn by means of maps, charts, and pictures.

KN
CO
AP
2. Make a piracy time line. Where possible, illustrate it to show examples of the ships that were used, the clothes that were worn, and the treasures that were sought or taken.

AN
SY
3. Do some research to learn how pirates have promoted settlement in certain parts of the world and the ways in which they have influenced place-names, language development, and customs in these areas.

Name _____

A Strange Calling

Piracy was not a respected occupation, and it was fraught with danger. This risky and illicit business was a strange calling. What made men leave the safety and relative comfort of their homes on land for the uncertainty and hardship of life on the sea?

A variety of economic, social, and personal factors encouraged piracy. As in any age, some men preferred to obtain their living by theft, rather than by honest work. A number of these men became pirates because they thought they would have a better chance of eluding capture. Other men turned to piracy in desperation when they lost their jobs during economic depressions or as a result of the Industrial Revolution, which swept Europe during the eighteenth century.

Another factor that encouraged piracy was a series of laws passed by the English Parliament beginning in 1651. Called the Navigation Acts, these laws were designed to force the American colonists to trade their raw materials for British manufactured goods. Their purpose was to create a shipping and trade monopoly in which the colonies would be economically dependent upon their mother country. But the demand for goods imported from other countries was so great in the colonies that the pirates who captured these goods on the high seas and the smugglers who brought them ashore operated with the express consent of both colonial governors and influential merchants.

Two additional factors that also encouraged piracy were the lack of effective means of communication and the absence of international laws against this form of robbery. Crews of ships under attack by buccaneers had no way to call for help. Acts of piracy often went unreported for days or even weeks while plundered ships limped into port. By the time a ship's owner learned that he had been victimized, the pirates had long since vanished and could not be found for punishment or revenge. And even if these bloodthirsty brigands could be located, there were no international laws against piracy under which they could be prosecuted. Thus, for a time, piracy was not only a strange calling but, for some, a lucrative one as well.

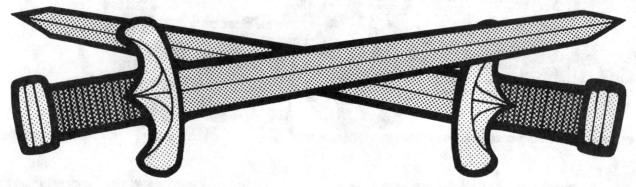

Activities

KN
CO
1. Today, the word **pirate** is used in reference to manuscripts, audio and video tapes, and computer software. What is the meaning of the verb **pirate** when it is used this way?

KN
CO
2. One way in which sailors were obtained for pirate ships and other vessels was by **shanghaiing**. Look up this word to discover where it came from and what it means.

KN
CO
AP
3. Do some research to find out what laws have been passed to prevent piracy and punish pirates. Make a time line showing both the dates and the most important provisions of these laws.

AN
SY
EV
4. Find out more about the provisions and effects of the Navigation Acts. What were some of the goods which the colonists wanted or needed to obtain from countries other than England? In what ways were these acts, or laws, beneficial to the colonies? to England? In what ways were they harmful to the colonies? to England? Were they fair to the colonists? Why or why not?

Name _____

The Pirate Articles

Even cutthroats needed rules to survive. Seemingly lawless pirates were governed by a very strict code called the **Pirate Articles**. When a sailor joined the crew of a pirate ship, he had to sign these articles and swear over an ax or a Bible that he would obey them at all costs.

Although the rules varied somewhat from ship to ship, they were generally democratic and were designed to prevent an individual or small group from gaining too much power. The captain was usually elected by popular vote. He was chosen for his knowledge of the sea and his leadership capability, rather than for his battle skills. He reigned supreme only during an attack and stayed in power only as long as his raids were successful. His share of the booty was usually twice that of the other crew members; but between raids, he had to eat the same food they ate and endure the same hardships they experienced.

When pirates captured a merchant vessel, they automatically **impressed** surgeons and carpenters, forcing them into service aboard the pirate ship. Pirates gave other members of the captured crew **quarter**, meaning that they invited these sailors to become pirates, too. Crew members who declined were usually allowed to sail on after all cargo had been removed from their vessel, but sometimes they and the ship's passengers were taken prisoner and later set free on shore, where a passing vessel could rescue them.

The Pirate Articles governed the disposition of captured booty. Usually, it was divided equally among members of the pirate crew, but there were exceptions. The captain received twice as much as the other sailors. The man who first sighted the merchant ship was rewarded, perhaps with the best pistols captured aboard or with an extra share of the booty. A pirate who lost a limb in battle also received an extra share of the take.

According to the Pirate Articles, theft of one crew member's share of the booty by another crew member was punishable by **marooning**, that is, abandonment on a deserted island with little hope of rescue. Desertion was punishable by death or marooning. The murder of one pirate by another could be punished by tying the murderer and the corpse together and throwing them overboard. Lesser crimes and disputes were brought before the quartermaster, who often settled them by means of a fair fight between contestants on shore.

The Pirate Articles
(continued)

Because sailing vessels were made of wood and could burn easily, the Pirate Articles contained strict rules governing the use of candles, lanterns, and fires aboard ship. Smoking and open flames were usually prohibited below deck, and fires for cooking were permitted only in calm weather. Sailors who broke these rules experienced the application of **Moses' Law,** a painful punishment in which thirty-nine strokes or blows were administered on a man's bare back with a whip or rod.

Pirates generally agreed to a "no prey, no pay" policy. This policy made their lives ones of feast or famine. When they found unprotected merchant vessels loaded with valuable cargo which proved to be easy prey, they had good food to eat and more money than they could spend. But when they had trouble finding ships or capturing them, their rations dwindled, and they received no pay.

Although the Pirate Articles varied somewhat from ship to ship, they served to unite the members of each pirate crew and to provide them with an organizational framework and a means of ensuring safety and settling disputes during long months at sea.

Activities

AP 1. Members of a pirate crew suddenly find themselves without a captain. Believing that none of them is qualified to take over, they decide to advertise in the hope of filling the vacancy. They come to you for help. Design a brochure, flier, newspaper ad, or poster for them. In it describe the available position and list all of the important qualifications for the job.

AP 2. Create a mural of a pirate ship accosting a merchant vessel.

AN
SY
EV 3. In some ways, the social organization aboard a pirate ship could be classified as a mini-democracy. In other ways, this organization contradicted everything a democracy stands for. Explain.

Name _____

A Pirate by Any Other Name

Basically, a **pirate** is a sailor whose livelihood is derived from looting ships on the high seas or from plundering coastal towns. Throughout history, however, pirates have been known by a variety of other names. Some of these names have glorified or romanticized their deeds, while others have spelled out exactly what these cut-throats were up to.

During the golden age of piracy, pirates were sometimes more politely referred to as **sea dogs** or **sea rovers**. Pirates have also been called brigands, picaroons, and swashbucklers. The English word **brigand** comes from older French and English words meaning "to fight" and "one who fights." A **brigand** is one who lives by plunder, usually as a member of a band. The English word **picaroon** is derived from the Spanish word *pícaro*, meaning "rogue." A **rogue** is a wandering and dishonest person who is inclined to mischief or worse. A **swashbuckler** is a boasting soldier or a blustering daredevil.

One French word for pirate is *corsaire*, from which came the English word corsair. The **corsairs** were Muslim pirates who operated along the Barbary Coast of Northern Africa. These Barbary pirates, as they were also called, sailed the Mediterranean Sea, plundering ships, raiding coastal cities, and taking captives back to Africa to be sold as slaves.

Buccaneers were Dutch, English, and French seamen who lay in wait for treasure-laden Spanish galleons sailing from ports along the northern coast of South America or plying the waters of the Caribbean Sea.

During the seventeenth century, some pirates were called **privateers**. These pirates were actually commissioned by the monarch of one country to sail their armed ships against warships and commercial vessels of other countries.

One of the Dutch words for pirate is *vrijbuiter*, from *vrijbuit*, which literally means "free booty" or "something of value which is taken by force." It is from this name for pirate that the English word **freebooter** comes. The Spanish word for freebooter is *filibustero*. During the mid-nineteenth century, this term was applied especially to American military adventurers who encouraged uprisings in Latin America.

Brigand, corsair, freebooter, picaroon, privateer, sea dog, sea rover, or swashbuckler—a pirate by any other name is still a sea robber, a thief.

swashbuckler * picaroon
corsair * sea dog * brigand
buccaneer * freebooter

Activities

KN
CO

1. Today, the word **filibuster** is used in reference to something that happens during debate in a legislative assembly. Find out what **filibuster** means when it is used in this way and explain how this meaning of the word is related to its derivation.

CO
AP

2. Create a pamphlet for seventeenth- and eighteenth-century merchant vessel operators in which you give them ten tips on how to protect themselves and their ships from being attacked and plundered by pirates.

Name _____

All Aboard

Pirates shared their ships and worked for nobody in particular other than themselves. They elected a **captain** from among their ranks, usually someone superior in knowledge of the sea and in bravery. But, in reality, the captain had little authority. Only during battle could he exercise absolute authority. At other times, major decisions were made by a show of hands, and the captain could as easily be voted out as in. His only special privilege was a double share of the loot acquired in a raid.

Next to the captain, the **quartermaster** was the most important man on any ship. Like the captain, he could be elected or deposed by a majority vote of the crew. The quartermaster looked after the interests of crew members and was empowered to punish such minor offenses as failing to care for one's weapons or quarreling aboard ship. For these infractions, he might administer a flogging if this punishment was sanctioned by majority vote of the crew. The quartermaster was first to board a captured ship, and it was his job to divide the plunder.

Pirate ships also had the usual man-of-war officers if they were able to find them. The **lieutenant's** main function was to take over if the captain was killed in battle. The **sailing master** was in charge of setting the sails and steering the ship. The **boatswain** cared for the boat's tackle and supplies, and the **gunner** took charge of shipboard weapons and gun crews.

Other valuable men to have along were a carpenter, a sailmaker, and a surgeon. The surgeon really had little capacity to treat the main causes of death in the tropics—malaria, dysentery, and yellow fever. He dressed wounds and performed amputations during battle, a job which the carpenter often took over in the absence of a surgeon, because the tools of these trades were similar. Some pirate ships even had a group of musicians whose job it was to entertain the crew while they were at sea and to demoralize the enemy during battles.

Activities

KN CO AP 1. All members of the pirate crew were expected to do their share of work aboard ship. Draw a large poster-sized diagram of a sailing ship of the day. Label the diagram and make a list of the jobs that had to be done in order to keep the ship afloat. Use appropriate terminology for jobs related to working the sails.

KN CO AP 2. Sailors had to **careen** their ships from time to time to recaulk seams, burn off barnacles, or replace ruined planks. Find out more about this hazardous business. Draw a picture of a ship being careened and list the steps necessary to get the job done.

Name _____

Life Aboard Ship

The picture that comes to mind when we hear the word pirates is actually a combination of the factual attributes of some notorious pirates and of the fictional details that are presented in such accounts of pirate life as *Treasure Island*, *Peter Pan*, and *Captain Blood*. In truth, there is often a wide gap between the glamour of fiction and the glare of reality. For example, in the movies, pirates are depicted as elegantly dressed swashbuckling cavaliers who wear gold earrings and brandish shiny daggers. Yet, more often than not, pirates were a dirty, disheveled, drunken lot with few clothes to wear and little money to spend.

In the movies, pirate ships are freshly painted and grandly rigged; but real pirates ships were dingy, dirty, and infested with vermin. Pirates sloshed their decks with vinegar and salt water or with captured brandy in an effort to disinfect and disinfest them. Pirates also fumigated their living quarters with burning pitch; but during long voyages, nothing could be done about the rats and cockroaches, which multiplied uncontrollably.

Diseases and death were unwanted passengers aboard every pirate ship. The crews for pirate vessels often consisted of double or even triple the number of hands required to sail the ships. These sailors were packed into the vessels like sardines in cans. They slept side by side in quarters that were dark and damp, cramped and musty. Because of poor sanitation and crowded conditions, they suffered from a variety of ailments, including colds, dysentery, malaria, scurvy, typhoid, and yellow fever.

Thirst and starvation were constant threats to pirate crews. On long voyages, supplies of fresh water and edible food dwindled. Drinking water, which was stored in barrels or casks, became stagnant. Meat and fish quickly rotted because there was no refrigeration. Bread and biscuits were always infested with weevils. On the rare occasions when a pirate crew captured a well-stocked ship, the food and drink aboard that ship were considered as valuable as any of the other booty.

Name _____

Life Aboard Ship
(continued)

Unlike the elegant buffets pictured in pamphlets advertising today's cruise ships, the meals served aboard yesterday's pirate ships were monotonous and unappetizing at best and unhealthful or even poisonous at worst. Much of the food was cooked on deck in a gigantic cauldron. One meal that was prepared in this way was **salmagundi**. This souplike dish could be made from nearly any meat that was available—chicken, duck, fish, ham, pigeon, or turtle. The meat was simmered in water to make a stock. To this stock were added cabbage, pickled herring, hard-boiled eggs, grapes, and a generous amount of wine. Before serving, the mixture was seasoned well with salt, pepper, garlic, oil, and vinegar. Fortunately, pirates frequently dined in the dark so they could rarely see what they were eating!

Most of the time, life aboard a pirate ship was unclean, uncomfortable, and unsafe. The dangers and discomforts to be endured were many, and the rewards were few.

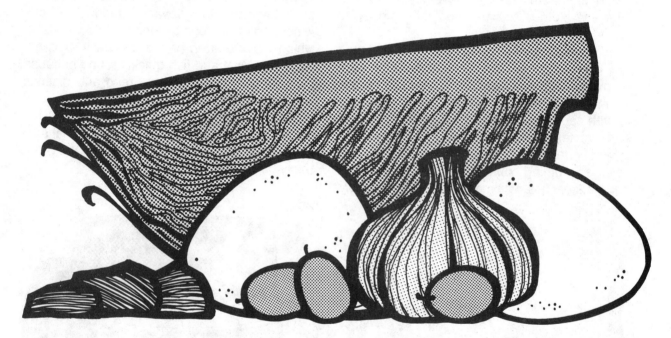

Activities

KN
CO
AP
1. Though most pirates were illiterate, imagine that you are a pirate who is able to write. Create several diary entries in which you detail the day-to-day struggles you and the rest of the crew face aboard ship. End this series of entries with a description of a successful foray against a merchant vessel.

KN
CO
AP
2. Many of the diseases from which pirates suffered were caused or aggravated by the shipboard diet, which was limited to foodstuffs that could be carried aboard, bought, caught, or captured. For example, **scurvy** is caused by a lack of ascorbic acid. Do some research to learn the symptoms of scurvy, the food sources of ascorbic acid, and why British sailors came to be called **limeys**.

KN
CO
3. Pirates are sometimes referred to in literature as a "scurvy" lot. What does the word **scurvy** mean when it is used in this way?

CO
AN
SY
EV
4. Do some research to discover what "remedies" were used to treat common ailments aboard pirate ships. Compare them with the treatments prescribed for the same ailments today. In what ways are they similar? In what ways are they different? Which ones are most successful? Why?

Name _____

Pirate Ships

Pirates prized speed and power in the boats they used. Their particular favorites were light, fast, maneuverable vessels from which they could easily prey upon the more sluggish merchant ships that were used to carry cargo.

The **schooner** was the ship used primarily by pirates in North American and Caribbean waters. This vessel had two masts, a narrow hull, and a shallow **draft**, which allowed the pirates to hide in remote coves and to navigate shallow shoreline waters. The schooner carried a crew of seventy-five and was outfitted with eight cannons and four swivel-mounted guns.

The **three-masted square-rigger** was also a suitable pirate vessel. Although it was not as swift as some other ships of its day, it was large and relatively stable, and proved to be unusually seaworthy on long voyages. A crew of two hundred could easily be accommodated aboard this ship, which was armed with twenty or more cannons and many swivel-mounted guns. The large cargo capacity of this ship made it ideal for transporting the booty, or **swag**, of a pirate fleet.

Smugglers and coastal pirates favored the **sloop**. The swiftness of this ship made it ideal for surprise attacks on unsuspecting merchant vessels. A sharp **bowsprit** nearly as long as the boat itself enabled this craft to carry more canvas, or sails, than other boats, thereby making it more nimble. The sloop could easily maneuver in the channels and sounds where the merchant ships that were its prey sought refuge.

The **brigantine** was the vessel most pirate captains preferred to use as their combat craft. With ten cannon mounts and a crew of one hundred, it was a very effective attack ship.

Activities

KN
CO

1. Unlike the large ships of today, the ships used by pirates were made of wood. Look in an encyclopedia or large dictionary to find a diagram of the principal parts of a wooden sailing ship. Familiarize yourself with the way a ship of this type was built and rigged.

KN
CO
AP

2. The average pirate ship carried a huge arsenal of weapons. Among these weapons were **blunderbusses** with folding bayonets, **boarding** or **rigging axes**, **cannons**, **cutlasses**, **daggers**, **muskets**, **pistols**, and **rapiers**. Do some research to discover what you can about the appearances of these and other pirate weapons. Then create a chart on which you name, describe, and picture each one.

Name _____

Commercial Vessels

The commercial vessels, or **merchantmen**, that pirates preyed upon were usually much larger and heavier than the pirate ships. For example, the **East Indiaman** was a sailing ship that traveled to the East Indies and the Orient. It was 160 feet long and carried a crew of up to three hundred. This Dutch craft had space for more than fifty cannons, but rarely carried even half that number because cannons were heavy and took up valuable cargo space. Because the East Indiaman moved slowly when sailing under a full load of cargo and was seldom adequately armed, this ship was especially vulnerable to attack by pirates, who sought to waylay it as it carried Eastern treasures back to Western home ports.

Another merchantman was the Dutch **flute**, a broad-beamed, flat-bottomed cargo carrier that was inexpensive to build, cheap to man, and had half again more cargo capacity than other ships of similar size. Flutes were among the favored prey of pirates because they usually carried a very small crew—sometimes as few as twelve—and a very large cargo.

Yet another vessel that fell victim to pirate raids was the **three-masted, square-rigged merchant ship** of the late seventeenth and early eighteenth century. This craft could make the trans-Atlantic crossing from Europe to America in four weeks and was well equipped to accommodate both passengers and cargo. Though pierced for up to sixteen cannons, it rarely carried more than a few because of the relatively small size of its crew.

Activities

KN CO
1. Look at a map of the world or at a globe and chart the courses European merchant ships might have followed to reach ports in the Orient or along the Spanish Main and return home with their cargoes of coins, ceramics, fabrics, gems, precious metals, spices, and lustrous woods.

KN CO AP
2. The following words are used to name some part or to describe some characteristic of a ship: **boom**, **bow**, **bowsprit**, **bumpkin**, **draft**, **jib**, **mast**, **stern**. Use these words to start a picture dictionary of maritime terms. Print each word on a separate sheet of paper. Beside the word, show in parentheses how it should be pronounced. Below the word, write its definition or description. Then, write a sentence in which you use the word. Finally, on the bottom half of the sheet of paper, draw and label a picture that will help you remember what the word means. Punch three holes down the left-hand side of each one of these sheets and tie them together with yarn or place them in a three-ring binder. Add a new page to your dictionary each time you encounter another unfamiliar maritime term.

Name _____

Pirate Chasers

Pirate ships were not the only vessels roaming the high seas for the purpose of combat. For example, the British Royal Navy had some very potent **pirate chasers** captained by men who were determined to rid the world's shipping lanes of the pirate scourge. The crews of these ships were combat trained, and the ships themselves were outfitted for battle.

Among these pirate chasers was the navy's **sloop**, which was bigger and more heavily armed than the pirate sloop. Another was the **man-of-war**, which was comparable to the large three-masted, square-rigged merchant ships. This vessel frequently "rode shotgun" for cargo convoys, and its presence and size were often enough to scare off would-be attackers. Navy **snows** typically carried a crew of eighty and differed very little from square-rigged brigantines; but the set of their sails gave them additional speed, making them capable of mounting successful attacks against roving pirate ships.

Activities

KN
CO
1. At the top of a large sheet of paper or a piece of poster board, print the title **Purposes and Characteristics of Ships**. Divide this sheet or board into three columns. Label these columns **Merchants**, **Navy**, and **Pirates**. At the top of each column, print the word **Purposes**. Below this word, list the specific purposes of this group. Below the purposes, print the words **Characteristics of Ship** and list the characteristics that a ship used by this group would need to accomplish the group's purposes at sea.

KN
CO
AN
SY
EV
2. At the top of a large piece of poster board, print the title **Ships of the Seventeenth and Eighteenth Centuries**. Divide the board into four columns. Label the left-hand column **Characteristics**. Above the other three columns, print the word **Ships**. Then label these three columns **Merchant**, **Naval**, and **Pirate**. Divide each ship column into two or three parts and label each of these subcolumns with the name of a particular merchant, naval, or pirate vessel. In the left-hand column, list such characteristics as **Length**, **Width**, **Tonnage**, **Draft**, **Crew Size**, **Cargo Capacity**, **Passenger Capacity**, **Armaments**, **Maneuverability**, and **Speed**. Then look up each vessel in an encyclopedia or in a book about piracy or ships and record all of the information available for each vessel in the appropriate column and rows. Compare these ships on the basis of what you have learned in your research. In what ways were they similar? In what ways were they different? Which one was the largest? Which one was the fastest? Which one was most maneuverable? Which one was most heavily armed? Which one had the best combination of characteristics for use as a merchant vessel? for use as a pirate chaser? for use as a pirate ship?

Name _____

Jolly Roger

It has always been customary for a ship to fly the flag of the nation in whose service or under whose commission or protection it is sailing; however, pirate ships were not ruled by law or custom. They sailed under the flag of no nation. Instead, for centuries, pirates devised their own flags, which were meant to strike terror in the hearts of their intended victims.

Each pirate captain designed an emblem to represent his vessel. In doing so, he made use of a variety of commonly recognized symbols. For example, a white skull and crossbones on a black background was one symbol for death. This symbol first appeared as a motif on pirate flags around 1700, when the French pirate Emanuel Wynne used it in combination with an hourglass to signify to his intended victims that death was fast approaching and that their time was running out. Other symbols used on pirate flags were crossed or brandished cutlasses, daggers, bleeding hearts, skeletons, and devils.

The name **Jolly Roger** was commonly given to the pirate flag. Though the origin of this name remains a mystery, it may have come from the French words *joli rouge*, meaning "pretty red," and may have been used to describe the blood-red banners flown by early privateers to signal that they would give no quarter to members of a captured crew.

Activities

KN
CO
AP

1. Pretend that you are a pirate captain. Design a flag to represent your ship and crew by cutting simple symbols from red or white construction paper or felt and gluing them to a black background of similar paper or fabric.

AP

2. Draw and label a detailed picture of the ship you will use for your escapades. Remember to give your ship a name.

AP
AN

3. You will need a crew to assist you. Make a list of the men you hope to persuade to join you. In this list, include descriptions of the specific positions you will be filling and lists of the characteristics you will be looking for among the applicants for these positions.

Name _____

Parrots and Eye Patches

Colorful legends have long been a part of pirate lore. Sometimes an isolated incident was romanticized in a painting or book of the day and gradually came to symbolize the characteristics and customs of pirates as a whole. **Walking the plank** was one such incident. The popular legend has pirates forcing blindfolded victims to walk a plank extended over the side of a ship until they lose their balance and fall to a watery grave. Actually, there is only one known instance of this practice aboard a real pirate ship. While it is true that any prisoner who displeased his pirate captors might be summarily pitched overboard to the sharks, it is only in paintings and movies that we find these offenders being regularly made to walk the plank.

There is also little evidence to support the many tales of **buried treasure**. Booty was nearly always divided equally among the pirates on board ship. The buried treasure myth is based largely on a rather isolated instance in which Captain Kidd buried his swag on Gardiners Island, near what is now Long Island, New York. When Kidd was subsequently jailed, the British recovered the booty and sent it to England. Blackbeard is reported to have buried treasure near Ocracoke Inlet, North Carolina; but this report has never been supported by a find. Treasure is rumored to be buried along coastlines around the world, but neither facts nor finds have substantiated these rumors.

Other popular legends include the keeping of pet parrots, the wearing of a single gold earring, the wearing of a bandana tied about the head, the use of eye patches and peglegs, and a penchant for rum. Eye patches and wooden legs are possibilities, given the battles that were fought, the weapons that were used, and the lack of surgical skills of most shipboard doctors of the day. The liking for rum is probable, considering that most other drinks, including fresh water, were hard to come by and harder to store for any length of time.

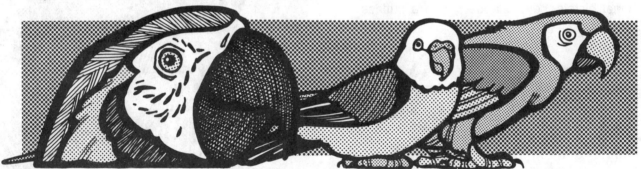

Activities

KN CO AP
1. You have come across a yellowed pirate map indicating the location of buried treasure. After secretly gathering together a small crew you believe you can trust, you head for the remote coastline indicated on the map. Keep a journal of your feelings throughout your search for treasure with emphasis on your mounting excitement as the probability of great wealth increases.

KN CO
2. Success! Your shovel strikes something hard, and frantic digging unearths a chest containing booty captured by the famed pirate, Blackbeard. Describe in detail the treasure contained in the battered sea chest. List each item and estimate its worth today.

KN CO
3. Do some research to learn more about modern-day searches for the aging treasure carried aboard sunken merchant and pirate vessels. How does one go about organizing and financing such a search? How does a searcher know where to look? What skills or talents must searchers have? What special equipment do they use? How much does a search of this kind cost? If treasure is recovered, to whom does it belong? Share what you learn with other members of the class.

Name _____

Blackbeard

The British pirate known as Blackbeard was born Edward Drummond and later changed his name to Edward Teach, or Thatch. Teach honed his pirating skills as a British privateer in the West Indies during the War of Spanish Succession. After this conflict was over, he became one of the most famous and ferocious pirates in history.

Teach's physical appearance was legendary. He was tall, enormously strong, and had a wild look about him. His trademark was a long and bushy beard, which reached from his eyes to his chest. He braided strands of it into pigtails and tied them with colorful ribbons. Two of these braids stuck straight out above his ears.

Before Blackbeard went into battle, he put the ends of long, lighted matches under his hat so that his terrifying face would be framed in a wreath of smoke and flames. To enhance his demonic appearance, he dressed entirely in black and wore a saber and a bandolier with three braces of pistols loaded and ready to fire. On a wide belt around his waist, he wore additional pistols, some daggers, and a cutlass.

Name _____

Blackbeard
(continued)

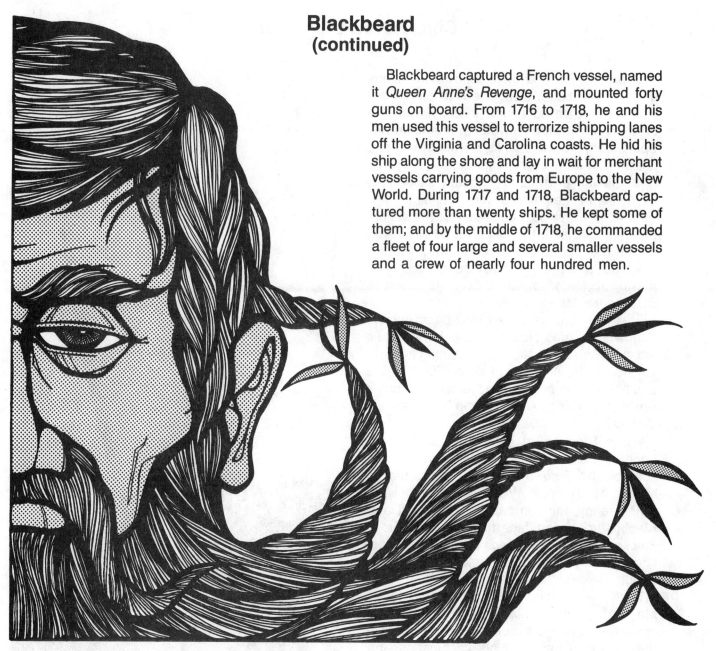

Blackbeard captured a French vessel, named it *Queen Anne's Revenge*, and mounted forty guns on board. From 1716 to 1718, he and his men used this vessel to terrorize shipping lanes off the Virginia and Carolina coasts. He hid his ship along the shore and lay in wait for merchant vessels carrying goods from Europe to the New World. During 1717 and 1718, Blackbeard captured more than twenty ships. He kept some of them; and by the middle of 1718, he commanded a fleet of four large and several smaller vessels and a crew of nearly four hundred men.

Activities

KN
CO

1. Shel Silverstein has written and illustrated a marvelously imaginative poem called "Captain Blackbeard Did What?" which is a humorous speculation about what might have happened had this notorious cutthroat ever shaved off his full and wiry beard to reveal a weak chin. This poem appears on page 152 in *A Light in the Attic* (New York: Harper & Row, 1981). Find a copy of this book and enjoy the poem.

KN
CO
AP

2. Blackbeard probably was constantly in need of able-bodied men to assist him in his piracy. Compose a help-wanted ad to aid Blackbeard in his search for men with just the right qualifications.

KN
CO
AP

3. Most pirates flew their own flags or banners on their ships. These flags were designed to frighten anyone coming in view of the ship. Do some research to learn more about these flags. Then design one to represent the exploits of Blackbeard. Consider using black construction paper and white chalk to achieve the proper effect.

Name _____

Blackbeard's Demise

Between 1716 and 1718, Blackbeard nearly destroyed shipping along the American coast from the Carolinas to Virginia. In fact, Blackbeard created so much havoc that Alexander Spotswood, the lieutenant governor of Virginia, posted a reward for his capture.

In the fall of 1718, Blackbeard sailed into Ocracoke Inlet along the North Carolina coast with two of his ships. Spotswood seized the opportunity and sent two ships—the HMS *Pearl*, under the command of Lieutenant Robert Maynard, and the HMS *Lyme*, under the command of Midshipman Baker—to capture Blackbeard "dead or alive."

These two ships followed Blackbeard into the narrow inlet, thus blocking his getaway. Once the exit was sealed off, a terrible battle ensued. For hours, the pirates and sailors fired bullets and homemade hand grenades at one another. Baker was killed, and his ship was severely damaged.

When Blackbeard believed that most of Spotswood's men were dead, he and his men boarded the *Pearl*, and the two crews met in hand-to-hand combat. With cutlasses and pistols at the ready, the two captains, Maynard and Blackbeard, stood face to face. Both fired. Blackbeard's shot missed. Maynard's hit his target, but had little effect. Blackbeard continued to fight fiercely.

Finally, with a mighty blow, Blackbeard broke Maynard's cutlass in two, leaving him defenseless. As the seemingly victorious pirate drew back to finish off his vanquished and helpless foe, one of Maynard's men slashed Blackbeard's throat. Still the giant pirate fought on. While other crewmen shot and slashed at him, he grabbed yet another pistol from his belt; but as he readied it to fire, he slowly gave in to his wounds and slumped onto the deck, dead.

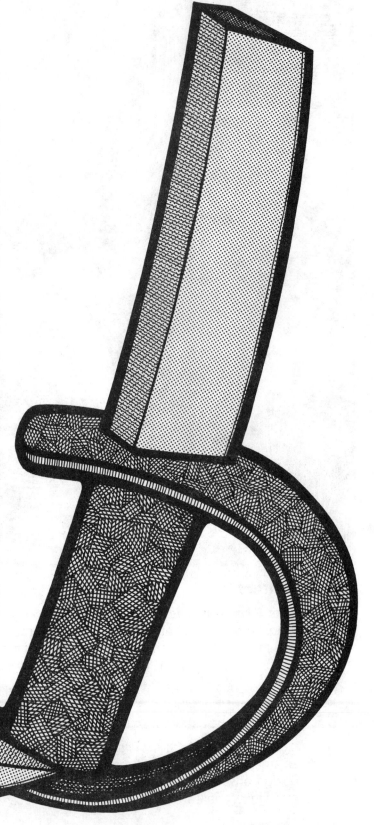

Name _____

Blackbeard's Demise
(continued)

When the curious sailors examined Blackbeard's lifeless body, they discovered that he had been variously wounded at least twenty-five times. With their leader dead, Blackbeard's pirate crew cast down their weapons and surrendered to Maynard.

As a lesson to other pirates, Maynard ordered that Blackbeard's head be cut off and hung from the bowsprit of the *Pearl*. Legend has it that, when Blackbeard's headless body was thrown overboard, it swam around the ship several times before sinking to its final resting place in the ocean depths.

Blackbeard's repeated successes along the American coast had encouraged other pirates; but after his demise, coastal piracy all but came to an end.

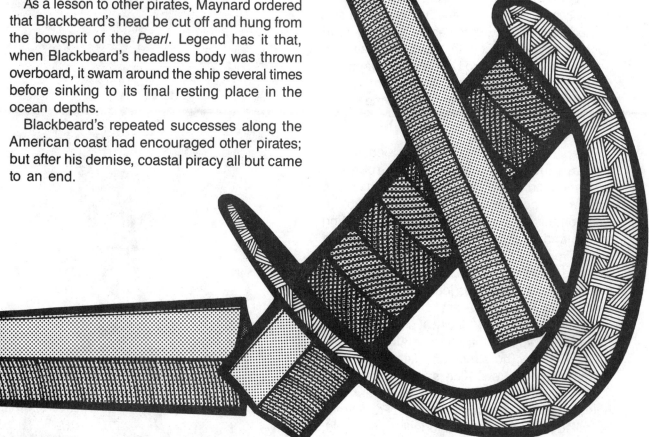

Activities

KN CO AP   1. Design a wanted poster resembling the one Lieutenant Governor Spotswood might have distributed in his attempt to capture the infamous Blackbeard, dead or alive.

KN CO AP   2. In accounts of the exploits of colorful characters such as Blackbeard, it is often difficult to separate fact from fiction, life from legend. Write your own account of a real or fictional event in Blackbeard's life. In your account, mix elements of both life and legend.

AN SY EV   3. During the battle that resulted in Blackbeard's death, this pirate apparently fought on long after he had been mortally wounded. Newspapers and history books are replete with accounts of brave men and women who, though seriously injured, have successfully defended themselves, unselfishly rescued others, or miraculously survived and found their way to safety. First, find and read an account of this kind. Then, list, analyze, and evaluate the personal qualities that enabled the central figure in this account to keep going even when the odds were against him or her and all seemed to be lost. Finally, compare this person with Blackbeard. In what ways are they similar? In what ways are they different? Are the actions of both persons heroic? Why or why not?

Name _____

Other Legendary Pirates

Blackbeard was only one of the famous pirates of the golden age. Many others left their mark on that period. One of the cruelest and most notorious was the Welsh buccaneer, **Sir Henry Morgan**. With the unofficial support of the British government, Morgan plundered throughout the Caribbean during the seventeenth century. With nearly two thousand buccaneers, he sacked and burned Panama City, then deserted his men and absconded with most of the booty. He was later arrested and returned to London, but eventually freed. King Charles II knighted Morgan and made him governor of Jamaica, where the former sea robber lived out his life as a wealthy and respected man.

Few pirates were as lucky. William Kidd, known as **Captain Kidd**, was born in Greenock, Scotland, and worked for years as a respectable New York trader and sea captain. In 1695, he was commissioned as a privateer by the King of England to seize pirates who were stealing goods from the East India Company in the Red Sea and the Indian Ocean. In his ship, the *Adventure Galley*, he began his journey. For almost a year, he sailed without any captures or other evidence of success. Unlucky at privateering, he turned to piracy off the coast of Africa. During a small mutiny, he struck and fatally injured a member of his crew. Kidd sailed to the West Indies, where he learned he had been denounced as a pirate and a murderer. From there, he sailed north again and reportedly buried gold, silver, and Indian goods on Gardiners Island near what is now Long Island, New York. When Kidd landed in Boston, he was arrested and sent to England to be tried for piracy. He was found guilty and hanged.

The tales and legends about Kidd's supposed buried treasure have made him inseparable from the swashbuckling hero of page and screen. The "Ballad of Captain Kidd" became a popular song, and western literature recalls Kidd's deeds and those of other sea robbers in such works as Edgar Allan Poe's "The Gold Bug" and Robert Louis Stevenson's *Treasure Island*.

Other Legendary Pirates
(continued)

Pirates were a colorful lot. Captain Bartholomew Roberts, or **Black Bart** as he was known, was a courageous fighter who wore finely tailored clothes, a plumed hat, a gold chain and cross around his neck, a sword at his side, and two pairs of pistols on the end of a silk sling over his shoulders. Proper and gentlemanly, he forbade drinking, gambling, and swearing aboard his vessel. No pirate could match his incredible career. The entire Atlantic was his hunting ground. In fewer than four years, Bart captured more than four hundred vessels. Bart always showed mercy toward his victims and was considered one of the greatest pirate captains of the golden age. Fellow pirates called him "pistol proof," meaning that he was expert in handling his ship and crew during battles and skillfully eluded injury or capture. But, as successful as Black Bart was, he was shot and killed during a raid before he was forty years old.

Other colorful characters include Jack Rackam, or **Calico Jack**, whose name came from the bright cotton clothing he wore as he plundered about in the West Indies. He was captured and hanged. **Charles Vane** wrecked his vessel on an uninhabited Caribbean island. When he was finally rescued by a passing ship, he was recognized as a pirate and was hanged.

Name _____

Other Legendary Pirates
(continued)

Stede Bonnett, a retired Army major, wore a powdered wig and fine clothes, but was a bungler when it came to piracy. His days as a pirate ended when he was caught and hanged. **Edward England** was a scourge in both Caribbean and African waters but unusually kind toward his prisoners. His kindness proved to be his undoing. He was deposed as pirate captain for freeing a captured merchant captain and died a beggar on Madagascar.

History even records the terrible deeds of two female pirates. **Anne Bonney** and **Mary Reade** fought in the Caribbean, every bit as fiercely and fiendishly as their male counterparts. Both dressed like men to win places on pirate crews. Their trail of killing ended with their capture off the coast of Jamaica in 1720. Both were thrown in prison, where Mary died of fever. No records exist of Anne's demise.

Jean Laffite spent years pirating and smuggling before turning patriot during the War of 1812 to aid the United States in the Battle of New Orleans. No pirate was more famous during his own lifetime than English Captain **Henry Every**, who was also known as John Avery, or Long Ben Avery. He became the central figure in a popular play at London's Theatre Royal and the prototype for Captain Singleton in Daniel Defoe's novel entitled *The Adventures of Captain Singleton*. Every's legendary wealth encouraged many to try piracy, but he died penniless.

Activities

KN CO
1. Make a large chart of facts about famous pirates. For each pirate, include his or her name, nickname or alias, years of birth and death, location of piracy, most infamous deeds, and a brief description of how his or her life ended.

KN CO
2. On an outline map of the world, label the locations of major pirate activity throughout history. Indicate years of activity and names of principal characters involved.

Name _____

Correlated Activities

Language Arts

KN CO AP Create a word search or crossword puzzle to challenge your friends. Use the following words and add more pirate terminology of your own:

brigand	privateer
buccaneer	salmagundi
corsair	sea dog
cutthroat	seafarer
freebooter	sea rover
picaroon	swashbuckler

KN CO AP EV Make an annotated bibliography about piracy for use by classmates who want to learn more about this subject. Find ten books or articles about pirates and/or piracy in your personal, school, or community library. Create a bibliographic entry for each book or article. In each entry, include the following information: (1) the author's name with the last name first, (2) the title of the book or the title of the article and the name of the periodical or larger volume in which it appeared, (3) the name of the publisher, (4) the year in which the book or article was published, (5) a brief summary of the information presented in the book or article, and (6) your opinion about how well this information is presented and about how valuable this source is. Alphabetize these entries on the basis of the authors' last names.

Science and Technology

AN SY Though the pirates that once roamed the high seas in search of vulnerable merchant ships have all but disappeared, a new kind of pirate, or freebooter, is in the news today. The modern-day Blackbeard is involved in the unauthorized copying of computer programs, records, cassettes, or video tapes. In this way, he or she obtains the material at a very low cost and avoids having to pay a copyright fee; however, he or she also deprives the artists and authors of their royalties and the producers of compensation for the time and money they have invested. Compare these modern media thieves with the seafaring pirates of the past. In what ways are they similar? In what ways are they different? Which pirates would you prefer to confront? Why?

Social Studies

AP AN Both trading companies and nations sought to end piracy. Pretend that you live during the golden age of piracy and that you have been hired by one of these groups to put an end to this scourge. List ten steps you would take to make the seas a safer place for both passenger ships and merchant vessels.

buccaneer · sea dog

brigand · salmagundi

cutthroat · seafarer

Name _____

Posttest

Circle the letter beside the best answer or the most appropriate response.

1. One factor that encouraged piracy in the American colonies was the
   a. British Navigation Acts.
   b. European Industrial Revolution.
   c. worldwide economic depression.
   d. disappearance of the frontier.

2. The **Pirate Articles** were
   a. articles of clothing worn by pirates.
   b. a series of feature stories glorifying theft on the high seas.
   c. international laws against piracy.
   d. rules by which pirates lived.

3. Theft of one pirate crew member's share of the booty by another crew member was punishable by
   a. flogging.
   b. invoking Moses' Law.
   c. marooning.
   d. being made to walk the plank.

4. Muslim pirates who operated along the coast of North Africa were called
   a. buccaneers.
   b. corsairs.
   c. freebooters.
   d. privateers.

5. The **quartermaster** aboard a pirate ship usually did *not*
   a. punish minor offenses.
   b. board a captured ship first.
   c. divide the plunder.
   d. dress wounds and amputate limbs.

6. Which of these common ailments could be prevented by consuming an adequate amount of ascorbic acid?
   a. dysentery
   b. malaria
   c. scurvy
   d. yellow fever

7. The **Spanish Main** is the name given to
   a. the Mediterranean coast of Spain.
   b. the Atlantic coast of Spain.
   c. the Caribbean coast of South America.
   d. the Atlantic coast of South America.

8. **Barbary Coast** is another name for
   a. the Mediterranean coast of Africa.
   b. the Aegean coast of Europe.
   c. the Mediterranean coast of Europe.
   d. the Atlantic coast of South America.

9. **Jolly Roger** was the name of
   a. a fearsome pirate captain.
   b. a pirate flag.
   c. the man who killed Blackbeard.
   d. a famous pirate ship.

10. Which one of these men was *not* a famous pirate?
    a. Daniel Defoe
    b. Edward England
    c. Henry Every
    d. Sir Henry Morgan

Answer Key

Pretest, Page 10		Posttest, Page 34	
1. b	6. a	1. a	6. c
2. b	7. d	2. d	7. c
3. b	8. d	3. c	8. a
4. d	9. a	4. b	9. b
5. b	10. c	5. d	10. a

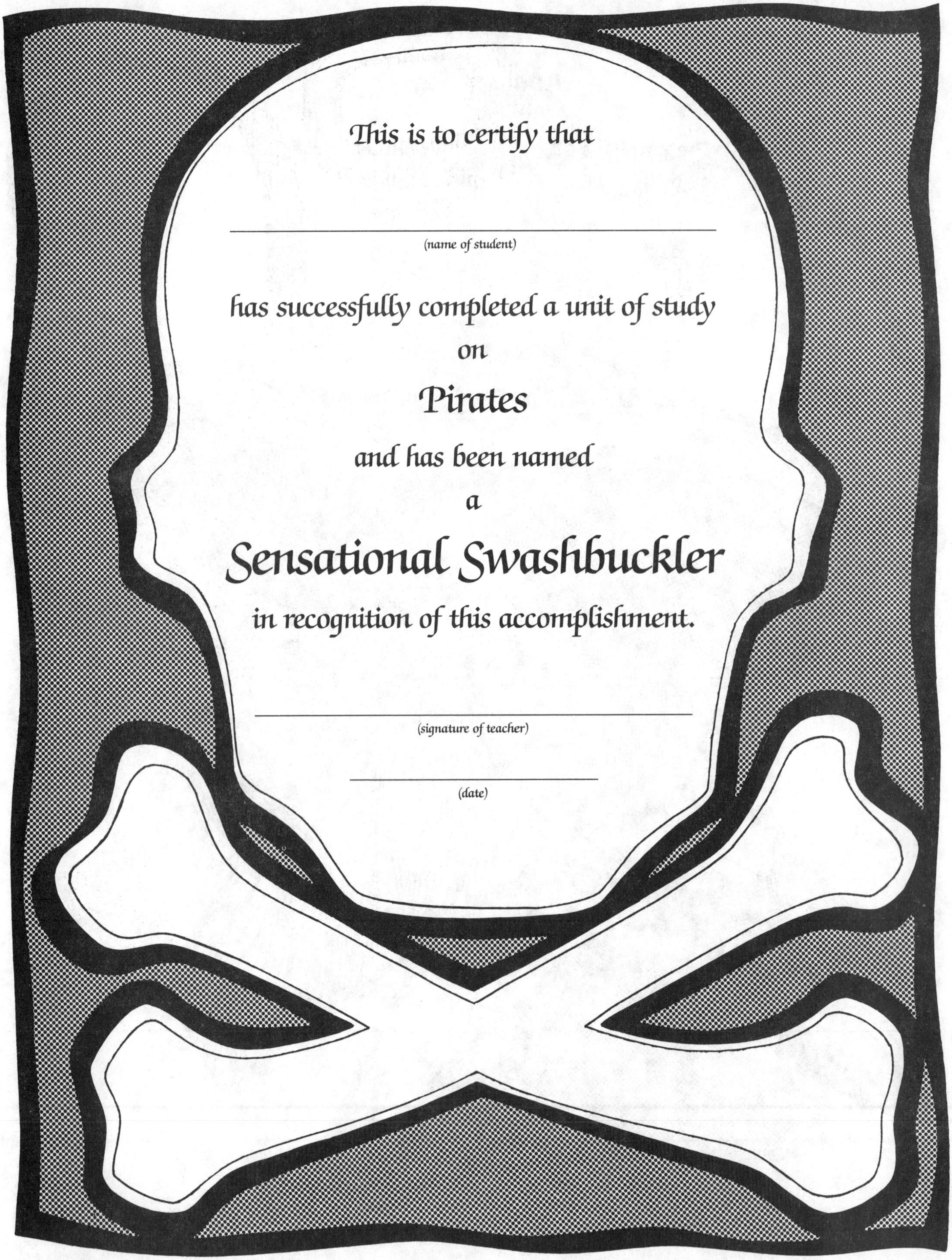

This is to certify that

_____

(name of student)

has successfully completed a unit of study

on

Pirates

and has been named

a

Sensational Swashbuckler

in recognition of this accomplishment.

_____

(signature of teacher)

_____

(date)

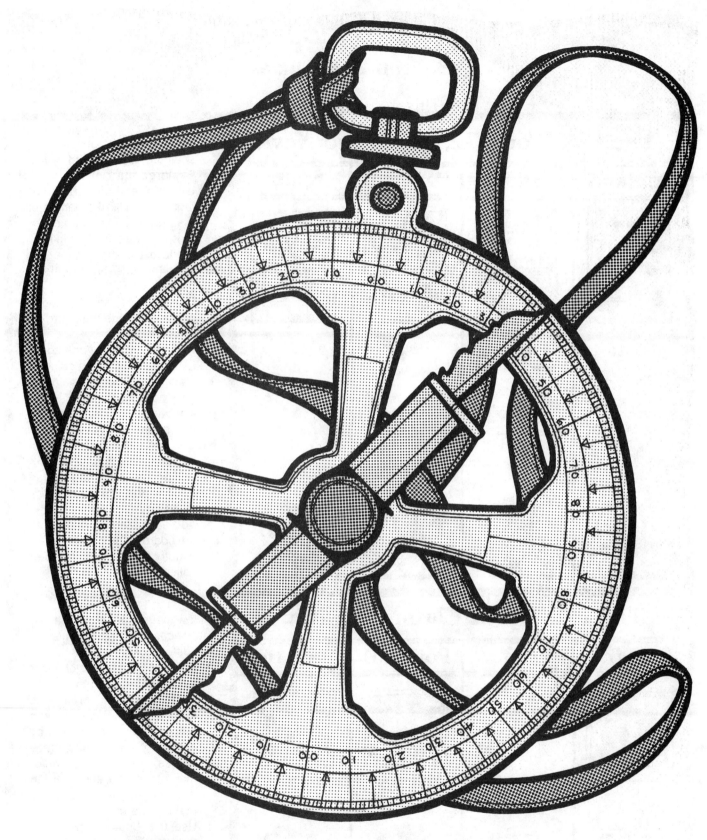

Explorers

Bulletin Board Ideas

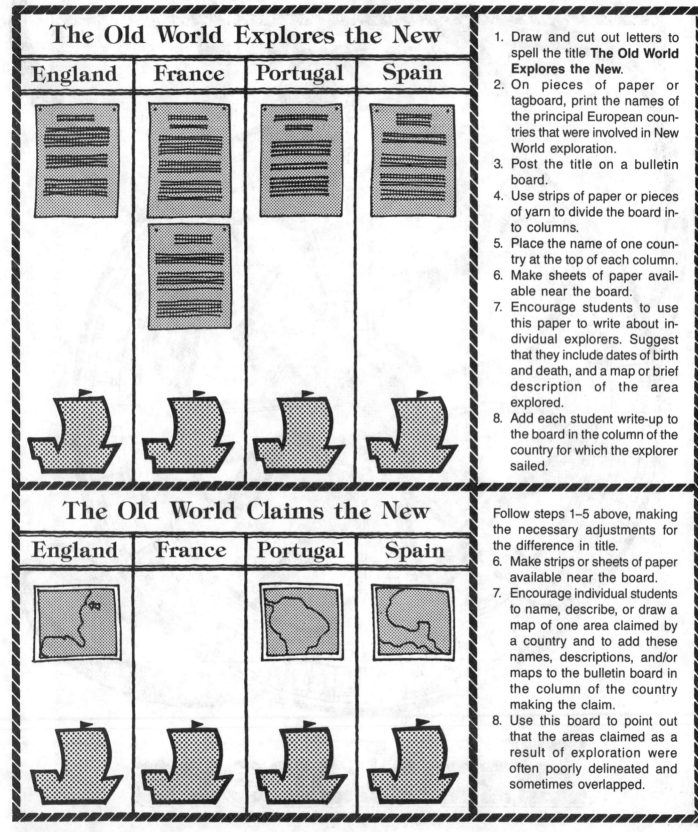

The Old World Explores the New

England	France	Portugal	Spain

1. Draw and cut out letters to spell the title **The Old World Explores the New**.
2. On pieces of paper or tagboard, print the names of the principal European countries that were involved in New World exploration.
3. Post the title on a bulletin board.
4. Use strips of paper or pieces of yarn to divide the board into columns.
5. Place the name of one country at the top of each column.
6. Make sheets of paper available near the board.
7. Encourage students to use this paper to write about individual explorers. Suggest that they include dates of birth and death, and a map or brief description of the area explored.
8. Add each student write-up to the board in the column of the country for which the explorer sailed.

The Old World Claims the New

England	France	Portugal	Spain

Follow steps 1–5 above, making the necessary adjustments for the difference in title.

6. Make strips or sheets of paper available near the board.
7. Encourage individual students to name, describe, or draw a map of one area claimed by a country and to add these names, descriptions, and/or maps to the bulletin board in the column of the country making the claim.
8. Use this board to point out that the areas claimed as a result of exploration were often poorly delineated and sometimes overlapped.

Learning Center Idea

Where in the World?

At this center you can

- Compare a map showing what people thought the world looked like in 1400 with a map showing what they know it looks like today.

- Trace the route followed by any explorer on a world map or globe.

- Use the map scale to calculate the distance sailed, ridden, or walked by an exploring party.

- Read articles about exploration and discovery.

- Read books about explorers' lives and adventures.

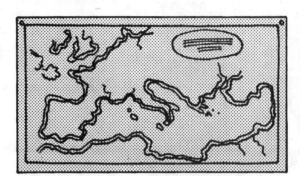

Name _____

Pretest

Circle the letter beside the best answer or the most appropriate response.

1. Viking ships were called
   a. galleys.
   b. biremes.
   c. long ships.
   d. caravels.

2. **Cathay** was another name for
   a. China.
   b. Japan.
   c. India.
   d. Persia.

3. Marco Polo was an ambassador for
   a. King Ferdinand.
   b. King Argon.
   c. Kublai Khan.
   d. Genghis Khan.

4. The Great Age of European Discovery began in the
   a. thirteenth century.
   b. fourteenth century.
   c. fifteenth century.
   d. sixteenth century.

5. Which one of these words does *not* name a sailing vessel?
   a. galleon
   b. caravel
   c. galley
   d. carrack

6. A **portolano** is
   a. a navigation manual illustrated with charts.
   b. an early astrolabe.
   c. a navigation map.
   d. an early compass.

7. The overland trade routes to China were controlled by
   a. Muslims.
   b. Spain.
   c. Portugal.
   d. England.

8. Under Prince Henry's direction, Portugal explored
   a. the Mediterranean coast.
   b. Africa's west coast.
   c. Africa's east coast.
   d. the North Atlantic.

9. The explorer who first rounded the southern tip of Africa was named
   a. Bartholomeu Dias.
   b. Pedro Alvares Cabral.
   c. Prince Henry.
   d. Vasco da Gama.

10. An explorer who found Florida while searching for the fountain of youth was
    a. Vasco Nuñez de Balboa.
    b. Alonso de Ojeda.
    c. Juan Ponce de León.
    d. El Dorado.

Name _____

The Vikings

The Vikings were skillful, daring seafarers from Scandinavia whose first explorations date back more than a thousand years. Also known as Norsemen or Northmen, they were among the best shipbuilders and the most skilled and fearless navigators in all of Europe. Their sleek, swift vessels carried them far from their home shores of Norway, Sweden, and Denmark.

At first, the Vikings sailed only as far as France and England, where they made lightning-fast raids on coastal communities, taking everything they could get their hands on. Eventually, their sense of adventure lured them even farther from their homeland.

The Vikings had no sophisticated instruments to guide them on long voyages, but their superior knowledge of the movements of the sun, stars, and ocean currents enabled them to navigate accurately without the aid of visible landmasses. For centuries, they traveled the rivers and seaways of Europe, and they worked their way westward across the North Atlantic, establishing settlements as far away as Iceland.

Under the leadership of Eric the Red, a band of Norsemen settled in Greenland in A.D. 985. Eric's son, Leif Ericson, is believed to have led the first white men to North America. In about A.D. 1000, Ericson sailed west to the present-day vicinity of Newfoundland and down the coast to the mainland of North America. He named the new land he had discovered "Vinland," or "Wineland," because of the many wild grapes he found growing there.

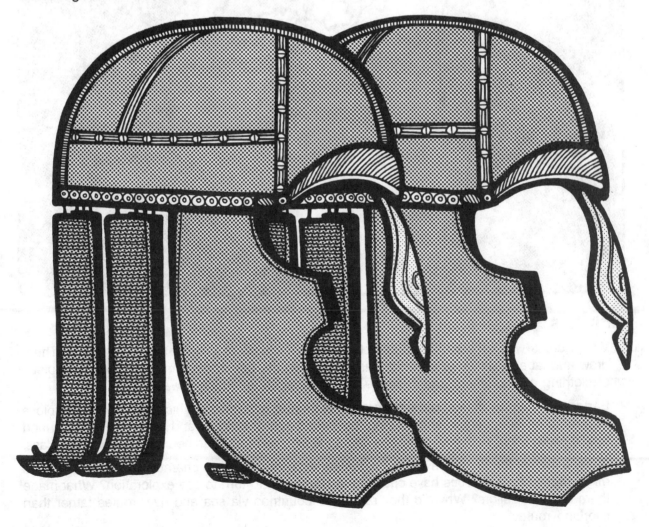

The Vikings
(continued)

When the Vikings returned from this voyage, their stories of the new land they had found excited others. A group of more than 150 men, women, and children traveled to Vinland to live. Hardships, including troubles with the Indians, forced them to abandon their settlement and return to Greenland. During the next 250 years, the Vikings made other visits to Vinland; but eventually they lost interest and abandoned their exploration of the area altogether.

Although the Vikings led the way to the New World nearly five hundred years before Columbus, their discoveries did not result in permanent settlements or generate widespread interest.

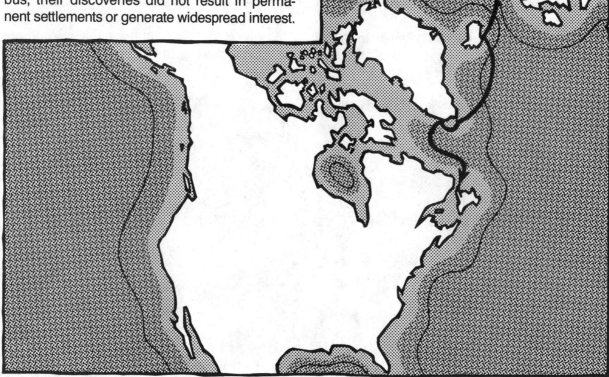

Activities

KN
CO
AP
1. Viking dress was very unusual. First, study some pictures of Vikings attired for battle. Then, draw and label a sketch of a Viking warrior. Explain the use and/or importance of each piece of clothing or equipment and describe the materials from which it was made.

KN
CO
AP
2. **Sagas** are colorful stories, passed from generation to generation, which describe the exploits of historic or legendary Vikings during the heroic age of Norway and Iceland. First, find and read a saga. Then, write your own saga about the exploits of a Viking hero. Share it with the class.

AN
SY
3. Study a map of the Scandinavian countries. Analyze their physical characteristics. In what ways might these characteristics have caused the Norsemen to turn to sea exploration? What made them become sailors? Why did they raid other countries via sea and river routes rather than overland routes?

The Viking Long Ship

The Vikings sailed the North Atlantic Ocean in open ships that were among the most well-constructed vessels of the day. Norse sagas tell of the sturdy, well-built vessels which carried adventuresome Vikings on countless sea exploits.

In 1880, when an actual Viking long ship was unearthed in Norway, historians were able to discover exactly what these remarkable ships looked like. They were small and shallow— usually about seventy feet long and sixteen feet wide. The long ship had a high prow and no keel. The hull, bow, and stern curved upward. Each ship had one large square sail and was propelled by oars. A small crew of thirty to forty sailors manned the ship. Colorful shields along the sides of long ships protected these oarsmen during a raid. The striped sail and a dragon figurehead gave sturdy Viking vessels their distinctive and impressive appearance.

Activities

KN CO 1. First, study several pictures of Viking ships. Then, draw and color a picture of one of them.

AN 2. First, do some research to learn how the Vikings constructed their ships. Then, list in chronological order the steps followed by the Vikings to build a long ship.

SY 3. Compare ships built by the Vikings with ships built in other regions of the world at approximately the same time. In what ways were they similar? In what ways were they different? What factors might account for differences in shipbuilding techniques in different parts of the world?

Marco Polo Visits the Far East

By far the most outstanding traveler and explorer to journey from Europe to Asia during the Middle Ages was a man named Marco Polo. He was by no means the first to travel the trade routes to the Far East, but the length and variety of his travels were mind-boggling. The primary importance of his travels lies in the fact that he chronicled them, describing in detail the people he had met and the lands he had traversed. *The Book of Marco Polo* created a sensation among Europeans, whose interest in faraway lands was just awakening.

Marco Polo was born around 1254 in Venice, Italy, one of the era's greatest seaports and trading posts. Merchants ran the town, and two prominent merchants were Marco's father, Nicolo, and his uncle, Maffeo. Marco was nearly sixteen years old when he first met Nicolo and Maffeo upon their return from a long journey to the Far East. They had established friendly relations with the great Kublai Khan in China. After hearing them tell of their adventures, Marco was eager to accompany them on their next journey.

In 1271, Nicolo, Maffeo, and Marco set out for China, or Cathay, as it was then known. They traveled by ship from Italy to the eastern end of the Mediterranean Sea and then spent nearly four years traversing the varied terrain of Asia to reach their destination.

Marco Polo Visits the Far East
(continued)

The Polos' journey took them through inhospitable deserts, cold mountain passes, interminable plains, and magnificent cities, such as Baghdad and Samarkand. Their caravan rode burros across the Hindu Kush, a mountain range in central Asia; camels across the Gobi, a desert in Mongolia and China; and horses across the plains. Even these remarkable experiences did not prepare Marco for his first glimpse of the great palace of Kublai Khan. Made of marble, the palace was decorated with precious jewels and gold, and furnished with rich carpets and fine furniture unlike anything Marco had ever imagined.

Marco described his journey to the Khan, who was so impressed by the young man's gift for remembering and reciting details that he made him an honored attendant and ambassador. For nearly seventeen years, Marco traveled the length and breadth of the Far East. During his travels, he saw many things that would not be commonplace in other parts of the world for centuries. The Chinese used paper money and, because of the scarcity of timber, burned "black stones" to heat water for the hot baths of which they were so fond. They had an organized system of mail delivery not unlike the American Pony Express. The Khan even kept warehouses of surplus grains for emergencies, such as famine or flood.

Marco Polo Visits the Far East
(continued)

Traveling through other parts of the empire, Marco saw polar bears and dogsled teams in Siberia, the land of the long winter nights. In the city of Hangchow, he saw a network of canals with more than twelve thousand stone bridges. He also saw factories and hospitals—all things that were unheard of in thirteenth-century Europe.

Around 1292, the Polos felt it was time to return to Venice. They received the Khan's permission to accompany a Mongol princess on her trip to Persia (now called Iran) to marry King Argon. This portion of their journey was no less exciting than what had gone before. They embarked with a fleet of fourteen ships and some six hundred sailors. These vessels were a wonder to the Polos. The largest of them had four masts and twelve sails, was three to four decks high, and had as many as sixty cabins. Together, this fleet of ships carried provisions for a two-year journey, and some decks housed earth-filled buckets in which grain was planted.

The voyagers sailed east across the East China Sea, past Japan and thousands of smaller islands. They stopped in Indochina (the peninsula that includes Burma, Democratic Kampuchea, Thailand, and Vietnam), where they viewed forests of ebony that grew to the water's edge. To avoid the monsoon season, they spent several months in Indochina. They visited Sumatra, the world's richest source of pepper and spices, and Java, where they beheld jungles with wild elephants, rhinoceroses, enormous vultures, and coconut trees.

After their visit to Indonesia, the Polos sailed on to Ceylon (now called Sri Lanka), where they observed pearl divers searching for oysters. Farther up the western coast of India, they saw crowded cities, panthers, white cows, vultures, hordes of bats, and multicolored parrots. Despite an encounter with pirates off the Malabar Coast, they arrived safely in Persia and eventually departed for Europe.

Marco Polo Visits the Far East
(continued)

In 1295, Nicolo, Matteo, and Marco Polo finally returned to Venice. But Marco's adventures were not yet over. Three years later, he was taken prisoner during a sea battle between Venice and Genoa. While in jail in Genoa, Marco Polo described his travels to a fellow prisoner, a well-known writer, whose *Book of Marco Polo* became very popular and was later translated into many languages.

Details of Marco Polo's adventures sparked European interest in Far Eastern goods. These goods were very expensive in Europe because of the difficult overland routes by which they were imported. Some enterprising merchants speculated that, if the great ocean of which Marco Polo spoke actually existed, then perhaps there was a way to travel to the Far East via an all-water route and a way to bring its treasured goods back so that they would be less costly.

This idea, along with Marco's descriptions of a far different life-style, inspired many would-be explorers. One who read these accounts with extraordinary interest was a man named Christopher Columbus.

Activities

KN
CO
1. Write several journal entries describing some of the wonders young Marco Polo encountered on the journey to China.

KN
CO
2. Draw pictures of five different types of transportation used by the Polos on their journey.

KN
CO
AP
3. Design a catalog featuring some of the wondrous foods, clothes, products, and inventions that Marco found in China. For each item, include a sketch and copy that describes how it looks and how it should be eaten, worn, or used.

AN
SY
4. Compare the culture that Marco Polo left behind in Medieval Europe with the one he found in China. In what ways were these cultures similar? In what ways were they different? What factors might account for the similarities? What factors might account for the differences?

Name _____

In Search of God, Gold, and Glory

The Great Age of European Discovery began in the 1400s. The Crusades had intensified the desire of people in Europe to learn more about the outside world. Constantinople and other Eastern cities were curiosities to Western crusaders. The palaces, beautiful churches, and paved streets they saw in these cities were unknown in Europe. Even more interesting to these crusaders were Eastern luxuries, such as silk, porcelain, gold, and jewels, which they carried back to their homelands.

Men who had been raised on a diet of little more than coarse bread and porridge became acquainted with new foods—apricots, lemons, melons, and rice. In an age when refrigeration was unknown, spices such as ginger, cinnamon, nutmeg, pepper, and salt were as precious as gold. These exotic flavors made less-than-fresh foods far more palatable.

Once Europeans became aware of Eastern products, they could not get enough of them. As the demand for Eastern goods increased, they became more and more costly to obtain. The Muslims, who controlled the overland trade, began to charge higher prices. As a result, European merchants were eager to bypass these traders. What was needed was a sea route from Europe directly to the Indies. Portugal and Spain led the way in trying to find such a route. Their expeditions launched the greatest period of exploration the world has ever known.

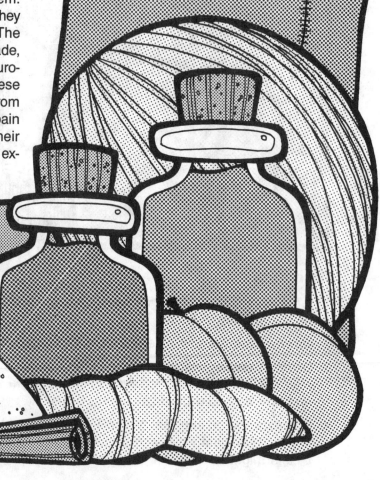

Name _____

In Search of God, Gold, and Glory
(continued)

Today, we have no doubt about the shape and size of the earth; and we have accurate maps of all its landmasses and oceans; however, during the period of early exploration, men actually had very little knowledge of what the world was like. The area around the Mediterranean Sea had been carefully explored and mapped, but beyond that lay a vast unknown. Unexplored areas became the objects of much speculation. For example, many people believed that the earth was flat and that, if a ship sailed too far, it was sure to fall off the edge! They told strange stories of terrible man-eating monsters, boiling seas, and mysterious kingdoms filled with peculiar half-human creatures. It took a particularly brave breed of men to venture out in the face of such frightening possibilities. But, for some, a desire for the riches that awaited the lucky adventurer outweighed the fear of what lay "on the other side."

Two qualities—courage and curiosity—have played a part in all great explorations. Combined with these laudable qualities, however, has been another, less noble one—greed. For some explorers, greed was the overriding reason for their ventures. These men were more greedy than curious and more brutal than brave. Whether the goal of exploration was to spread Christianity, to gain land, to conquer people, or to capture riches, the men who set sail into the unknown were a breed apart. They dared to extend the limits of the known world to each of its "four corners."

Activities

CO AP AN SY

1. Pretend that you are a member of the Chinese Travel Council trying to encourage East-West trade during the early 1400s. Prepare a brochure describing the journey an Italian trader might make to take his goods to China by an overland route. Include a map and a written itinerary listing alternative means of transportation and describing both the weather conditions and the road hazards one should expect along the way.

AN SY

2. Pretend that you are a would-be explorer. Prepare written arguments to present to a monarch to gain financial backing for your attempt to reach the East by sailing west. Be persuasive. Use all of the available knowledge of the day to convince him or her that your plan is a wise one.

AN SY

3. Compare a map of the known world before the Great Age of European Discovery with a map of the world today. In what ways are these maps similar? In what ways are they different? What factors might account for the differences?

Name _____

Life at Sea

Until the 1400s, most seagoing vessels were **galleys**, or **biremes**. These large ships had two banks of oars on each side and were used for traveling throughout the Mediterranean area. They were ill-suited for ocean travel, however, because the large number of rowers they required left little room for provisions or cargo.

In the early fifteenth century, an "all-sails" vessel called a **caravel** gradually replaced the galley as the foremost means of oceangoing travel. Caravels were light ships that were high-sided, broad, and deep, with a high forecastle in front and a still higher two-deck sterncastle at the rear. They had two or four masts and were usually equipped with lateen sails. Columbus's ships, the *Niña* and *Pinta*, were three-masted caravels.

The Spaniards had a more advanced version of the caravel known as the **galleon**. Galleons were larger than caravels and could carry more sail and more armament. A large galleon, called a **carrack**, was often used on longer ocean voyages. This ship carried three masts and square rigging. It was rounder, heavier, and better able to cope with strong ocean winds than smaller, lighter vessels. Columbus's flagship, the *Santa Maria*, was a carrack.

Life at sea was difficult. The men who went down to the sea in ships needed not only a sound vessel and an adventuresome spirit, but also great personal courage and physical strength. But never was there a shortage of men to answer the siren call of the sea.

Activities

KN CO
1. Describe some of the navigation methods and tools used by sailors of Columbus's time.

KN CO AP
2. Write a realistic account of life aboard the ship of a famous explorer. Discuss the dress, food, quarters, jobs, and tools, as well as difficulties like bad weather, disease, and loss of direction.

AN SY
3. Sailors who were preparing to undertake a voyage of exploration often experienced ambivalent feelings. They felt excited, but their excitement was frequently accompanied by a fear of the unknown. Describe these contradictory feelings and explain why both were justified.

Name _____

Mapping an Ever-Changing View of the Earth

Prior to the 1400s, there was little progress in the field of cartography. Medieval mapmakers, who were largely influenced by the Church, typically portrayed only three continents on a flat, disk-shaped earth.

As time went on, increased trading and shipping made possible a more accurate representation of the world. Maps were continually revised to reflect new information provided by ships' captains when they returned from their voyages in unknown or uncharted waters. In addition, on each major voyage sailed a cartographer, whose job it was to sketch the coastlines, harbors, inlets, and islands seen on the journey. This information enabled cartographers to improve existing maps and to create entirely new ones.

The development of printing made possible the production and circulation of multiple copies of maps. At first, maps were printed from carefully carved woodcuts. Later, their fine outlines were engraved on copper plates. In this process, the engraved plates were rubbed with ink and wiped dry so that ink remained only in the incised lines. A sheet of paper was then carefully smoothed against the inked plate, which resulted in a delicate reproduction of the original map on the sheet of paper. The existence of multiple printed copies made maps more readily available to those who needed them and more susceptible to correction by those who used them.

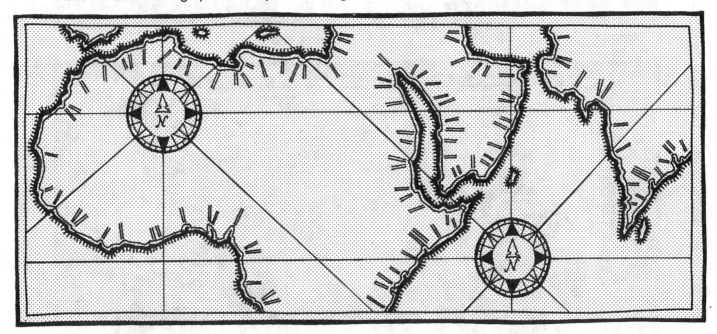

Activities

KN
CO

1. Do some research to learn about the contributions made by Ptolemy, Jocodus Hondius, Gerhardus Mercator, Abraham Ortelius, and Martin Waldseemüller to early mapmaking and the study of geography. Share what you learn with the class.

KN
CO
AP

2. Familiarize yourself with the following terms: **astrolabe**, **cartography**, **cosmography**, **Mercator projection**, and **planisphere**. Use these terms to start a picture dictionary. Print each term on a separate sheet of paper. Beside each term, show in parentheses how it should be pronounced. Below the term, write its definition or description. Then, write a sentence in which you use the term. Finally, on the bottom half of the sheet of paper, draw and label a picture that will help you remember what the term means. Punch three holes down the left-hand side of each one of these sheets, and tie them together with yarn or place them in a three-ring binder. Add a new page to your dictionary each time you encounter another unfamiliar term.

Portugal Takes a Chance

As East-West trade increased, Mediterranean and overland routes became more and more active. The Muslim and Italian monopolies on these routes caused prices for Eastern goods to soar. During the 1400s, other nations began to dream of finding their own all-water trade routes to Asia.

Portugal became the first Western European nation to search actively for such a route. The Portuguese were skilled at building and sailing ships, but they had not ventured far out to sea. Because Portugal did not possess a "window on the Mediterranean," the Portuguese had much to gain from finding an ocean route to Asia. In 1419, Henry the Navigator (the third son of Portugal's King John I), started a school at Sagres, Portugal, to train seamen for oceangoing exploration. He invited many scholars and mapmakers to assist him in this venture.

After careful study, Prince Henry theorized that an all-water route to Asia might be found by sailing south along the western coast of Africa and then east toward Asia. Henry sponsored many expeditions that followed this route. Members of each crew sailed as far south as they dared, drawing detailed maps and keeping written records. Before returning to Portugal, they erected a marker on shore to show how far south they had traveled. The challenge facing the next Portuguese captain was to sail even farther.

Although Prince Henry never actually went on a voyage himself, the expeditions he sponsored succeeded in mapping the west coast of Africa as far south as Sierra Leone. Under his direction, the Cape Verde Islands were discovered, and colonies were established on the Madeira Islands and in the Azores.

Activities

KN
CO
AP
AN

1. Prince Henry's step-by-step exploration of the western coast of Africa proceeded slowly, and rewards were meager. Describe the process by which the Portuguese gradually conquered the coastal route around Africa.

AN
SY
EV

2. Prince Henry's method of exploration earned him the nickname "founder of continuous discovery." Compare Henry's method of discovery with that practiced by other explorers of his day. In what ways were they similar? In what ways were they different? What factors might account for these similarities and differences? Which method or methods were most effective? Why?

Name _____

On to India

Prince Henry had concentrated on exploring along the west coast of Africa, and his work made Portugal increasingly hopeful of finding an all-water route to Asia. In 1487, a Portuguese explorer named Bartholomeu Dias set out to reach the southern tip of Africa. With a small fleet of ships, he sailed south as far as the mouth of the Orange River. There, a severe storm blew his ships far off course to the south. When the weather calmed, Dias realized that he was sailing east with no land in sight. Without knowing it, Dias had rounded the tip of Africa and entered the Indian Ocean; but his weary men forced him to turn back before he reached India.

Not long after Dias's voyage, Christopher Columbus sailed west across the Atlantic Ocean in search of the Indies. When he returned to Spain, many Europeans were convinced that he had reached the Indies, but some Portuguese were skeptical. Columbus had brought back none of the exotic products many Europeans associated with the Far East. These Portuguese still believed that the best route to Asia would be found by sailing around the continent of Africa. For this reason, nearly ten years after Dias had made his historic voyage, Vasco da Gama was sent by the king to sail all the way to Asia using the same route. The journey was a difficult one because of terrible storms and bouts with scurvy, but Da Gama pressed on. In November 1497, he finally rounded the Cape of Good Hope, as the southern tip of Africa had come to be known, and reached India in 1498. Prince Henry's theoretical all-water route to India had become a reality.

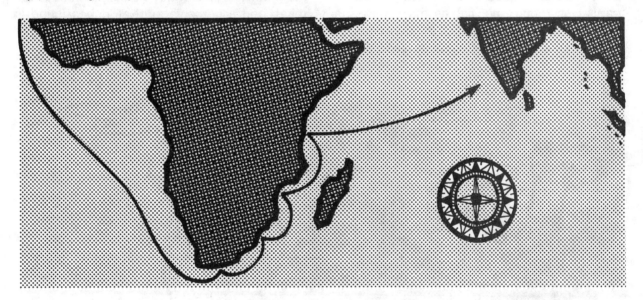

Activities

KN
CO
1. Columbus was present when Dias returned to Portugal. This Italian seaman and mapmaker was trying to persuade Portugal to back his westward venture. Explain why Dias's successful journey might have been a great disappointment to Columbus.

AP
2. Write a one-act play depicting Bartholomeu Dias's triumphant return to Portugal and Christopher Columbus's reaction to it. Use docudrama techniques. Base your play on facts but fill in as necessary from your imagination.

KN
CO
AP
3. Bartholomeu Dias was never really rewarded for the great part he played in Portugal's eventual discovery of a route to India. Though he supervised the building of Da Gama's ships, he was not included on that voyage. First, do some research to learn more about Dias's life. Then, write a biographical sketch about a part of his life or about some of his adventures.

Name _____

Christopher Columbus

Christopher Columbus was not the first European to find the New World. By the time he arrived, the Vikings had already come and gone. But the discoveries made by the Vikings went largely unnoticed outside Scandinavia. In contrast, the discoveries made by Columbus were discussed throughout Europe and aroused the interest of many Europeans in the New World. As a result, thousands of explorers and settlers soon followed where Columbus had led.

Columbus was born in the busy Mediterranean seaport of Genoa, Italy. He spent his youth watching great ships sail into port, unload their valuable Asian cargo, and then sail away. Later, he worked as a mapmaker in Portugal and read about the fantastic riches of the Indies that had been discovered and described by Marco Polo. Columbus concluded from his studies that the earth was round—not flat as many had supposed—and that the riches of the East could be reached by sailing west. Columbus also believed, incorrectly, that the Indies were only twenty-four hundred miles from Europe. While most geographers shared Columbus's belief that the earth was round, they did not agree with his estimate of the distance. Many of them suggested that the actual sailing distance from a European port to Asia might be as great as ten thousand miles. Neither Columbus nor the geographers realized that a giant landmass lay in the way!

Columbus wanted to test his theory, but putting together the needed exploratory expedition was a costly undertaking, one that required the financial support of the Crown. Columbus asked John II, king of Portugal, to sponsor his venture. At first, King John was interested, but later he refused because of the additional demands made by Columbus. The Italian seaman and mapmaker asked for three ships, the title of admiral, and a percentage of all riches found in new lands. In addition, he asked to be declared ruler of any lands he discovered.

Christopher Columbus
(continued)

While Christopher Columbus anxiously sought financial backing for his exploratory venture, Bartholomeu Dias rounded the southern tip of Africa, bringing the dream of an all-water route to the Spice Islands even closer to realization. Dias's success was very disturbing to Columbus, who was beginning to despair of ever having an opportunity to test his own theory.

Finally, Columbus found willing sponsors in King Ferdinand and Queen Isabella of Spain. At last, on August 3, 1492, he sailed from the port of Palos in Andalusia, Spain, with three ships and ninety sailors. After stopping in the Canary Islands to restock supplies of food, water, and live animals, Columbus and his crew set sail across the vast Sea of Darkness.

As the journey wore on, the men became increasingly fearful. Would they fall off the edge of the earth? Would they be devoured by sea monsters? Would their tiny ships be drawn into the maelstrom of boiling seas? Would they lose their way and never be able to return home? Discouraged and disillusioned crew members were secretly plotting mutiny when branches and leaves, a sure sign of land close by, were seen floating in the water. Finally, on October 12, seventy-one days after Columbus and his crew had left Spain, they sighted land.

Columbus thought he had reached the Indies described by Marco Polo. Decked out in shining armor, he and his men went ashore with the royal banner, planted it on the beach, and took possession of the new land they had discovered in the name of the King and Queen of Spain. The new land was actually an island in the Bahamas off the southern tip of Florida.

As Columbus and his men went ashore, they were met by people with reddish-brown skin. These people wore decorations of feathers and shells and brought their visitors fruit, vegetables, cotton thread, darts, and parrots. Columbus called these people Indians because of his belief that they were natives of the Indies he had been seeking.

Name _____

Christopher Columbus
(continued)

Columbus was not impressed by the fine climate and fertile soil of the new land he had discovered. He was determined to find the gold and riches he had originally sought. To this end, he wandered among the islands, giving them all Spanish names and raising crosses everywhere. When he asked the natives about the gold earrings they wore, they pointed toward the large island we now call Cuba and explained that "Cubanacan" was the source of their gold. Columbus thought they meant Kublai Khan and became even more convinced that he had found Asia.

When the *Santa Maria* was wrecked on Christmas, near the shore of Hispaniola, the sailors and natives moved the cargo onto the beach and used the timbers from the ship to erect Fort Navidad. Columbus left behind a year's supply of food and forty men while he returned to Spain with the remaining crew and ten Indians to spread the news of his discovery.

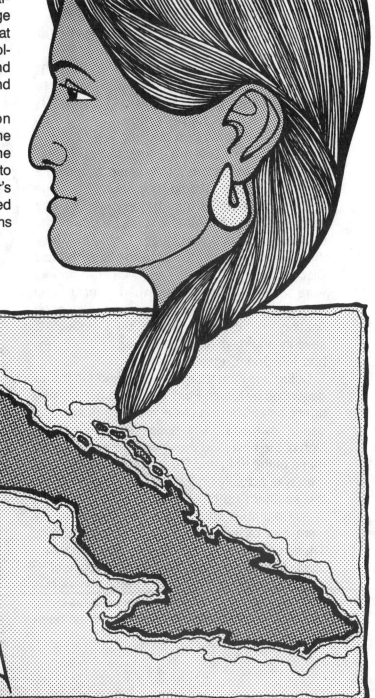

Christopher Columbus
(continued)

Columbus continued to lead voyages to the New World. On his second voyage, he brought twelve hundred settlers to begin Spain's first colony in the New World. On his third voyage, he actually set foot on the mainland of South America in Venezuela. His fourth and final voyage was an attempt to find a water passage through the mainland.

Two years after his last voyage, Columbus died without finding the riches he had sought. To the very end of his days, he remained convinced that he had landed in Asia. Although Columbus did not reach the East by sailing west, his discoveries were important because he opened the New World to Europe, he proved that sailors could cross an unknown sea and return safely, and he claimed vast new lands for Spain.

Activities

KN
CO

1. Do some research to learn what happened to Fort Navidad and to the forty men whom Columbus left behind on his first voyage to the New World.

KN
CO
AP

2. Make an illustrated time line of the outstanding events in the life of Christopher Columbus. Use at least three different sources for your information.

KN
CO
AP
SY

3. On a map of the world, trace the route Columbus believed he was taking to Asia. Then trace the route he actually took on his first voyage. Compare these two routes. In what ways are they similar? In what ways are they different? What factors might account for these similarities and differences?

KN
CO
AP
AN

4. Historians are not certain where Columbus first landed in the New World. In the past 194 years, at least nine different islands in the Bahamas have been proposed as the Italian explorer's landfall. Among these islands are San Salvador and Conception. First, locate these islands on a map of the Bahamas. Then, do some research to learn more about this controversy. On what evidence are the proposals based? Why is this evidence inconclusive?

Name _____ _____

England Makes a Claim

Portugal and Spain were not the only nations that sought all-water routes to the Indies. England also wanted to find a way to share the wealth. Thus it was that, in the spring of 1497, an Italian seafarer named John Cabot set sail for the Orient from Bristol, England. Believing he could reach the riches of the East by traveling west, Cabot sailed straight across the Atlantic on a route far north of that followed by Columbus on his earlier voyages.

After fifty-two days at sea, Cabot's ship, the *Mathew*, completed the rough North Atlantic crossing and landed on an island off the eastern coast of present-day Canada. Although no proof of Cabot's landing exists, historians now believe that the site was either Newfoundland or Cape Breton Island.

Cabot sailed farther south along the coast and was certain that he had discovered a new continent. In August, he returned to Bristol without gold, jewels, or spices. John Cabot had not reached the Indies, but he had claimed the mainland of North America for England and had prepared the way for the British colonization of that continent.

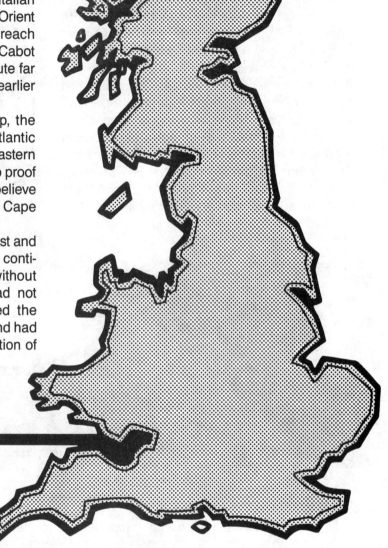

Activities

AP 1. Make a replica of the flag under which John Cabot sailed.

KN CO AP 2. From the time of Cabot until 1577, when Sir Francis Drake set sail, the English did very little exploring in the New World. First, read about Drake's journey around the world. Then, trace his route on a map or globe and write a brief chronicle of his travels.

KN CO AP 3. An English navigator named Henry Hudson made four separate voyages to North America in search of a northwest passage to the Far East. Sailing for the English Muscovy Company, for the Dutch East India Company, and then for a group of English entrepreneurs, he discovered both the Hudson River and Hudson Bay. Do some research to learn more about the northwest passage and about Hudson's voyages in search of it. Share what you learn with the class by means of a report and maps or charts.

Name _____

An Accidental Discovery

Serendipity is the faculty of finding valuable things by accident, when you are *not* looking for them. Pedro Alvares Cabral's discovery of Brazil was, indeed, both accidental and **serendipitous**.

In 1500, King Emanuel I of Portugal asked Cabral to take thirteen ships on a major expedition to the East along the route previously followed by Vasco da Gama. The purpose of this trip was to strengthen Portugal's commercial ties with the East Indies and to increase that Iberian country's landholdings.

While Cabral was sailing on a southwesterly course along the coast of Africa, he was forced off course in a westerly direction by wind and current, and accidentally landed on the coast of what is now the South American country of Brazil. On April 22, 1500, Cabral took possession of this new land in the name of his sponsor, the King of Portugal, and sent one ship to inform the Portuguese monarch of his claim.

After spending ten days anchored off the South American coast, Cabral once again set sail for the East Indies. As he and his fleet rounded the Cape of Good Hope, they were greeted by a terrible storm. Four of Cabral's ships were destroyed by the powerful winds and heavy seas. Among the crew members who lost their lives was Bartholomeu Dias, the commander of one of the ships in Cabral's fleet. Only a few years earlier, Dias had discoverd this cape and had aptly called it *Cabo Tormentoso*, "Cape of Storms." Dias's sponsor, King John, later renamed it *Cabo da Bõa Esperança*, "Cape of Good Hope."

En route to their destination, Cabral and his men discovered the large island of Madagascar. Eventually, they reached the Port of Calicut, India, where their efforts to establish a fortified trading post met with considerable resistance from entrenched Muslim traders. As a result, Cabral sailed farther south to a port where he and his men were better received. There, they traded European goods for Eastern spices.

In 1501, Pedro Alvares Cabral returned to Portugal. He had lost eight ships and many men, but he had succeeded in reaching India and in trading Western goods for Eastern ones. And he had discovered both Madagascar and Brazil. Although European sailors had preceded Cabral to the vicinity of the latter, South American country, Cabral was given credit for its serendipitous discovery.

Activities

KN
1. The word **serendipity** was coined in about 1754 by Horace Walpole, an English man of letters, to describe the good fortunes of the three princes of Serendip (a country now known as Ceylon). These young men, the heroes of a Persian fairy tale, discover agreeable or valuable things by accident, while they are looking for something else. Just for fun, find a copy of "The Three Princes of Serendip" and read it.

KN
CO
2. On a world map or globe, trace Cabral's probable route southwest along the western coast of Africa to Brazil, southeast to the Cape of Good Hope, northeast to the large island of Madagascar, and then farther northeast to Calicut (which is now called Kozhikode) on the west coast of India near that country's southern tip.

AP
3. Using the scale given on the map or globe, calculate the approximate number of miles Cabral and his men sailed from Portugal to India.

SY
4. Compare the approximate distance traveled by Cabral in the early sixteenth-century with the approximate distance an airline passenger would travel today to go from Portugal to India. Which distance is greater? By how much? Why?

Name _____

A Name for the New World

Other explorers followed Columbus, gradually making known the extent of the land he had discovered. In 1499, Alonso de Ojeda, accompanied by Italian navigator Amerigo Vespucci, explored the coast of Venezuela. In 1501–02, Vespucci directed another voyage, under the flag of Portugal, whose purpose was to follow up on Cabral's accidental discovery of Brazil. On this voyage, Vespucci explored the Brazilian coast and discovered the Río de la Plata.

Vespucci concluded that the landmass, which was thought by Columbus to be eastern Asia, was really a new continent. Vespucci based this conclusion on two ideas: (1) this new land bore little or no resemblance to earlier descriptions of Asia and (2) many European geographers rightly estimated that the distance around the world was much greater than the distance sailed by Columbus. In other words, although Columbus had sailed a great distance, he had not traveled far enough to reach Asia and must, instead, have reached some other land.

When Vespucci returned to Europe, he wrote and circulated letters describing his discoveries and detailing his ideas about the identity of this great land. A few years later, a German geographer and cartographer named Martin Waldseemüller gave Vespucci a permanent place in history by publishing his descriptions of the New World and by suggesting that it be called "America," a name derived from Amerigo, Vespucci's first name, in honor of this Italian navigator's accomplishments.

AMERIGO VESPUCCI

Activities

KN
CO

1. Martin Waldseemüller publicly suggested "America" as the name for the New World on an impressively large world map measuring some thirty-six square feet. Find out more about this map. When was it drawn? From what sources was the information it presented derived?

KN
CO
AP
AN

2. Waldseemüller later decided that Vespucci should not have received credit for the discovery of the New World; but because of mass printing and distribution, his map had been too widely circulated to be recalled for alteration or correction. So appealing was the name America that Gerhardus Mercator identified both a North America and a South America on the map of the world that he published in 1538. Thus, mass printing helped to popularize the name America. Consider and list some other possible effects that mass printing may have had on cartography, exploration, geography, and world trade and travel.

AN
SY
EV

3. Hold a debate on the topic "Resolved that the New World should be renamed in honor of its real discoverer, Christopher Columbus." Select two debate teams of at least three students each. Designate one team to argue in favor of the resolution and the other to argue against it and in favor of retaining the present name. Encourage team members to do research so that they are able to support their opinions with facts and to present their arguments within the structure of a formal debate, which includes both opening statements and rebuttals.

Name _____

The Fountain of Youth

Men sought many things in the New World. Among them were land, wealth, and power. But one man sought something different, a fountain whose waters could make old people young again.

The man who sought this fountain of youth was Juan Ponce de León. Born around 1460, Ponce de León sailed to the New World in 1493 with Christopher Columbus on that explorer's second voyage. For many years afterward, Ponce de León lived in the West Indies and searched, as others had before him, for gold. In 1508, he conquered Puerto Rico; and two years later, he became its governor. In 1511, he founded the Puerto Rican city of San Juan.

Ponce de León's unsatisfied urge to explore and his desire to escape the inevitable aging process led him to seek a very special fountain of which the Indians spoke. This fountain, which had the power to restore youth to those who drank its waters, was reputed to be on the island of Bimini. In 1513, Ponce de León set sail in search of this island with three ships. When he sighted what he believed was a large island, he dropped anchor off the coast and went ashore. Actually, the "large island" was the North American continent. Ponce de León named the land on which he walked Florida because he discovered it on Easter Sunday, which is called *Pascua Florida* in Spanish, two words that literally mean "flower festival."

Ponce de León explored much of the coast of Florida and made two futile attempts to establish a colony there. In 1521, during his second settlement attempt, Ponce de León was wounded in a battle with local Indians. He died later that same year.

Juan Ponce de León did not find the fountain of youth for which he searched nor the eternal spring its fabled waters were reputed to supply, but his discovery of Florida brought him immortality in the annals of history and opened this peninsula for later Spanish settlement.

Activities

KN
CO
AP

1. It is now believed that the idea of a fountain of youth actually originated in an Old World legend, which the Indians heard from earlier European explorers and repeated. First, find out more about this legend. Then, rewrite it in your own words.

KN
CO
AP

2. You are a sixteenth-century explorer in the Caribbean. You have heard about Ponce de León's unsuccessful quest for the fountain of youth but are still convinced that this fountain exists. Pretend that you find it, and write a diary entry, short story, or one-act play about what happens when you drink its miracle-working waters.

KN
CO
AP
AN

3. In 1565, Pedro Menéndez built a fort on the Florida coast to protect Spanish shipping interests there. Around this fort grew up the settlement of St. Augustine. Do some research to learn more about this oldest city settled by Europeans on the North American mainland. What did it look like then? How does it look today? In what ways does this city reflect its very special past? In what ways does it look to the future?

Name _____

A New World After All

Inspired by Christopher Columbus's accounts of sailing across the Sea of Darkness to find the Indies, a steady stream of Spaniards journeyed westward in search of the gold and riches they believed lay waiting for them there. Even though Amerigo Vespucci tried to persuade them that his was, indeed, a "new world" rather than a new way to reach the eastern part of the Old World, most of them remained unconvinced.

The Spanish attempted to establish colonies on the coasts of Colombia and Panama, but these expeditions met with disaster. In 1510, Vasco Núñez de Balboa united the remnants of these two groups of settlers to form the colony of Darien on the eastern shore of Panama.

Although Balboa is sometimes termed a conquistador, he rarely exhibited the cruelty that is characteristic of others who bear this title. Instead, he was usually kind and won the friendship of the Indians he encountered.

As governor of the region, Balboa sought to win favor with the Spanish monarch by claiming lands or finding wealth. In 1513, he left Darien with a party of two hundred and began an epic struggle through steaming, tangled jungles in search of a great sea described to him by the Indians. On September 25, from atop a mountain, Balboa first saw the broad, gleaming waters of the Pacific Ocean. After four more days of walking, he reached its shores. Exuberantly, he waded into the water, christening it the South Sea (because he and his party had actually walked south across the isthmus of Panama to reach it) and claiming it and all of the shores washed by it for the Spanish crown.

Balboa's discovery of a vast ocean beyond the American mainland confirmed Vespucci's assertion that Columbus had not landed on any part of Asia but had, instead, found a New World.

Activities

KN CO AP

1. What was the well-dressed Spanish explorer of the early sixteenth-century wearing? Draw and label the clothing and accoutrements that made up an explorer's wardrobe. Don't forget to include weapons and armor.

KN CO AP AN

2. Draw a map of the isthmus of Panama. On it mark the location of Darien. Then, trace the course Balboa and his men might have followed on their southward trek from this settlement to the Pacific. As a part of your research, determine the approximate distance between these two points in miles. Also, look up some typical temperature and humidity readings for this part of Panama on several days in late September. Record these numbers and dates on your map. List in order the types of terrain and the obstacles that Balboa and his men might have encountered on their epic march from sea to sea. Include in your list some indication of the changes in elevation to which these men would have been subjected.

KN CO AP AN SY

3. Balboa called the body of water he discovered the South Sea because he and his men walked south across the isthmus of Panama to reach it. Which explorer is usually given credit for naming this ocean the Pacific? In what year did he do so? What does this name mean? What is the approximate size of this ocean? What fraction or percentage of the earth's surface does it cover? With regard to size, how does it rank among the oceans of the world?

Name _____

A True Conquistador

Hernado Cortes was a Spanish adventurer, explorer, and warrior who both earned and typified the epithet conquistador.

Cortes was born in 1485, only two years before Dias sailed down the western coast of Africa toward that continent's southern tip and seven years before Columbus set a westward course to reach the riches of the East. As a young man of nineteen, Cortes sailed from his native Spain to the West Indies; and in 1511, he served as an officer under Diego Velásquez on that Spanish commander's successful expedition to conquer Cuba for Spain.

For a time after the conquest, Cortes lived the comfortable life of a wealthy conqueror on that Caribbean island; but he was not satisfied. In 1519, convinced that even greater riches could be his, Cortes set out with a small army of Spaniards to find the fabled Aztec Empire.

Cortes and his men sailed from Cuba to the Mexican coast. Once they were safely ashore, Cortes ordered that the ships in which they had made their crossing be burned so that his soldiers would be forced to fight for survival and would share his commitment to conquest.

For a time, Cortes trained and drilled his men rigorously. When he believed that they were ready, he led them toward the valley of Mexico and the great city of Tenochtitlán, heart of the Aztec world. Although this city housed as many as 150,000 to 200,000 people and the Aztecs were fierce warriors, they proved to be no match for the small band of well-armed and well-trained Spaniards. By 1521, the Aztec Empire had been destroyed. Montezuma, the Aztec ruler, was dead, and Tenochtitlán lay in ruins.

Unlike many New World explorers before him, Cortes succeeded not only in claiming territory but also in acquiring wealth. He conquered farmlands and captured rich stores of gold, silver, and jewels. Atop the ruins of the once-beautiful Aztec capital, he built Mexico City, the stronghold from which future Spanish expeditions moved either north, to invade what is now the United States, or south, to claim additional lands in Central and South America. And Cortes's success inspired many adventure-seeking Spaniards to abandon their efforts to reach the wealth of the East and, instead, to set sail for the New World and its riches.

Cortes was not only a seeker and a soldier, but also a conqueror, a ruler, and a leader in the Spanish conquest of America—a true conquistador.

Activities

KN CO
1. Mesoamerica, as Mexico and Central America are sometimes called, was the home of several distinct Indian cultures. Do some research to learn about the Olmecs, the Maya, the Zapotecs, the Mixtecs, and the Toltecs and about the common elements that characterized their cultures. Consider what contributions each one of these cultures may have made to the Aztec culture.

KN CO AP
2. Do some research to learn how each one of the following terms related to Mesoamerican culture: **atlatl**, **beans**, **cacao**, *chinampas*, **eagle**, **feathered serpent**, **maize**, **squash**, **stela**, **Teotihuacán**, **Tikal**, and **Tlaloc**.

KN CO AP AN SY
3. Both the Indians in Mesoamerica and the ancient Egyptians in Africa built pyramids. First, do some research to learn more about these impressive stone structures. Then compare what is known about the ways in which they were built and the purposes for which they were used.

Name _____

The South Sea Becomes the Pacific Ocean

After Vasco Núñez de Balboa's discovery of the South Sea confirmed that the Americas were a New World and not merely an eastern extension of the Old World, the European search for a water route to Asia centered on finding a way around or through this great landmass. Under the auspices of King Charles I (later, Emperor Charles V) of Spain, Portuguese navigator Ferdinand Magellan set out to find a more convenient way to reach the Spice Islands (also called the Moluccas), which he believed lay just west of Spanish America.

On September 20, 1519, Magellan sailed southwest from Sanlúcar de Barrameda, Spain, with a fleet of five ships and about 270 men. They reached the bay of Río de Janeiro on the southern coast of Brazil in December. As Magellan and his men journeyed down the eastern coastline of South America, looking for a passageway through or around that great continent, their ships were rocked and tossed by violent storms. Off the coast of Argentina, one ship—the *Santiago*—was lost in the angry seas.

At last, in late 1520, the remaining four ships reached the passageway from east to west. The crew of the *San Antonio* refused to navigate the treacherous waters of this narrow strait, so with only three ships, Magellan began a journey that lasted more than a month, from October 21 until November 28.

When Magellan finally reached what Balboa had called the South Sea, he found its waters so calm in comparison to the turbulent strait that he renamed it the Pacific, meaning "Peaceful." The waterway through which Magellan had sailed was later named the Strait of Magellan in his honor.

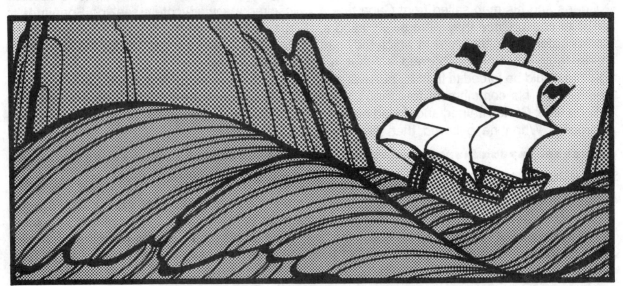

Activities

KN CO
1. On a world map or globe, trace Magellan's route southwest from Sanlucar de Barrameda, Spain, across the Atlantic Ocean to Río de Janeiro on the southern coast of Brazil, south along the eastern coast of South America, west through the Strait of Magellan, and into the Pacific Ocean.

KN CO AP
2. Using the scale given on the map or globe, calculate the approximate distance that Magellan traveled from Spain to the point at which he entered the Pacific Ocean.

KN
3. Magellan and his crew spent several months in a region of Argentina that they named **Patagonia**. Find out what this name means.

KN CO
4. A **strait** is a relatively narrow natural passageway connecting two large bodies of water. How many straits are there in the world? Name and locate some of them.

Name _____

Around the World in Many Days

As Magellan set sail across the vast Pacific, he thought that the Spice Islands were not far away. He had no way of knowing that it would be more than three months before he would see land once again. During this time, food and supplies ran out. Some of his crew members survived by eating sawdust, rats, and the leather from their shoes. Many crew members starved to death.

At last, in March 1521, Magellan and his weary men reached the island of Guam. After resting and obtaining fresh food and water, they again sailed west. On March 16, Magellan discovered the Philippine Islands. During his stay in the Philippines, Magellan unwisely allied himself with a treacherous native chieftain and was killed while on an expedition for this chieftain to the island of Mactan.

Leaving two of the three ships behind, the remnants of Magellan's crew headed home aboard the *Victoria* under the command of Juan Sebastián del Cano. After crossing the Indian Ocean and rounding the Cape of Good Hope, they reached Spain on September 6, 1522.

Although only eighteen members of Magellan's original crew survived and he was not among them, they are given credit for being the first to complete a voyage around the world. Their achievement forever laid to rest the question of whether the earth is round or flat and established the basis for vast Spanish territorial claims throughout the world.

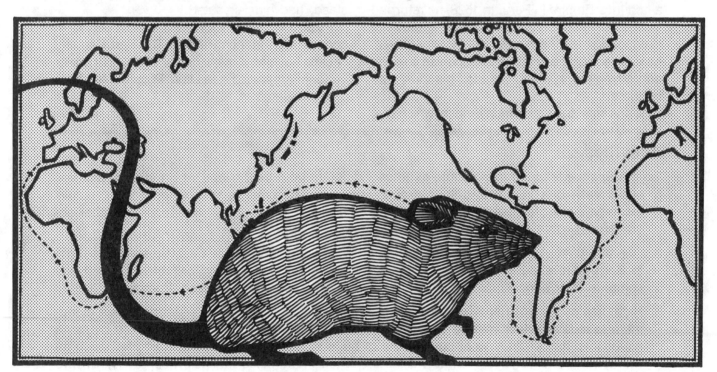

Activities

KN
CO
1. Do some research to learn the names of the five ships with which Magellan set sail from Sanlúcar de Barrameda, Spain, on September 20, 1519.

KN
CO
AP
2. Find out more about the circumstances surrounding the death of Magellan. Share what you learn with the class by means of a brief written report or a tape recorded message prepared in the style of a news broadcast.

KN
CO
AP
3. Imagine that you are a sixteenth-century journalist who was asked to accompany Magellan on his voyage. Write at least one article describing some portion of your incredible journey.

Pizarro Conquers the Inca

Balboa's discovery of the Pacific Ocean brought many Spanish settlers to Panama. During the first half of the sixteenth century, this tiny isthmus became an important center of power for Spain in the New World, and many Spanish expeditions set out from Panama to conquer parts of Central America.

It was also from Panama that the first Spanish invasion of South America was launched. The invading forces were led by Francisco Pizarro, one member of a Spanish family prominent in the early history of South America. Born about 1470, Pizarro came to America in 1509 and sailed in the Caribbean with Alonso de Ojeda later that same year. Pizarro settled for a time in Panama but became increasingly interested in rumors of a rich Inca Empire in Peru. In 1528, he returned to Spain and secured from Charles V authority to conquer and govern new territory. While there, he enlisted a force of some 180 Spanish soldiers and adventurers, which included his three half brothers.

At this time, the fabled Inca Empire, which was centered at Cuzco, Peru, dominated the entire Andean area from Quito, Ecuador, south to Rio Maule, Chile. This empire covered approximately 650,000 square miles. It had been forged from many smaller tribes and kingdoms into a single, closely knit state of six million people headed by an absolute monarch who ruled by divine right.

Pizarro returned to Panama in 1530 and began his campaign of conquest in 1531. For a time, fierce battles raged between the Spanish and the Inca. Then, in 1532, Atahualpa, the last Inca chieftain, was taken captive. He offered a room filled "once with gold and twice with silver" for his ransom. Although Pizarro accepted the riches, he refused to release Atahualpa and, instead, had him executed.

Pizarro's Spanish forces had succeeded in conquering the Inca Empire. The Peruvian city of Lima became a major center of Spanish power in South America. From Lima, Pizarro ruled Peru until his death in 1541.

Activities

KN
CO
AP

1. The Spaniards found Inca culture to be very different from their own. Draw and color pictures of two men—one dressed as a Spanish conquistador and the other as an Inca nobleman. Carefully research and accurately depict the clothing, hairstyles, jewelry, shoes, weapons, and other accoutrements that might have been worn or used by each.

AP
AN
SY

2. Like the Aztecs of Mexico, the Inca were an advanced Indian people. First, do some research to learn more about the Aztec and Inca cultures. Then, make a chart or table on which you compare their agricultural, architectural, artistic, religious, and educational practices.

CO
AP
AN

3. High on a spur in the Peruvian Andes stands Machu Picchu. This now-deserted city is a monument to Inca architectural and engineering genius. It featured terraced gardens fed by stone aqueducts. Its buildings were constructed of huge stones, some of which weigh as much as twenty to fifty tons. These stones were transported many miles from the nearest quarry and were carefully cut so that they fit together so tightly that not even the thinnest knife blade can be placed between them. The mystery of Machu Picchu is that the Inca moved its massive stones without horses, carts, or even the wheel and shaped these stones using only other stones. First, find out more about Machu Picchu. Then, offer a theory that explains how the Inca, who were virtually a Stone Age people, were able to build such a remarkable complex.

AN
SY

4. Just for fun, learn about the villages built in modern times on the steep slopes of the Himalayas by the Sherpas of Tibet. Compare these villages with those constructed by the Inca on similar mountain slopes five hundred to a thousand years earlier. In what ways are they similar? In what ways are they different? What factors of climate and culture might account for these similarities and differences?

Name _____

The Land Conquers a Would-Be Conqueror

Hernando de Soto, a Spanish nobleman, had joined Pizarro on his conquest of Peru. But De Soto had befriended Atahualpa and had been so disgusted by the Inca chieftain's execution that he returned to Spain in 1536. Still hungering for adventure, De Soto secured from Charles V approval to conquer Florida, the land discovered earlier and claimed for the Spanish crown by Juan Ponce de León during his unsuccessful search for the fountain of youth.

De Soto was eager to conquer Florida because he had heard the Indians describe it as a "land of gold." In 1539, he set out from Spain for Tampa Bay with ten ships, 350 horses, and one thousand men. For three years, De Soto and his party wandered in the wilderness of southeastern North America. During this time, they went north through what later became the states of Florida, Georgia, and the Carolinas into Tennessee. Then they turned south into Alabama, where De Soto was wounded in a battle with an Indian tribe.

Undeterred by his own wounds or by the losses of battle, De Soto continued his futile search for gold. In May 1541, he and his party sighted the Mississippi River and became the first white men to view the "Father of the Waters." But the land De Soto had hoped to conquer eventually conquered him, and he died of a fever in 1542. To ensure that the Indians would not learn of his death, De Soto's men attached weights to his body and dropped it into the mighty Mississippi.

Though De Soto never found the gold and silver for which he searched or a wealthy Indian tribe whose land and people he could conquer, his quest for both made him the first European to explore much of the southeastern part of North America.

Activities

KN
CO
1. On a map of the United States, trace the approximate route followed by De Soto and his men in the southeast.

AP
AN
SY
2. De Soto was born in the Extremadura Province of Spain. This region was nicknamed the "cradle of conquistadors" because it was also the birthplace of Balboa, Cortes, and Pizarro. Do some research to learn about the environment and the history of this region. What factors and events might have combined to produce so many men with adventuresome spirits?

Name _____

In Search of El Dorado

Inspired by Indian legends and the tales of Cabeza de Vaca, another Spanish explorer, Francisco Vásquez de Coronado led an expedition through the southwestern part of North America. In 1540, Coronado traveled north from Mexico to find the fabled wealth of the Seven Cities of Cibola. For two years he searched, accompanied by some three hundred Spanish soldiers, hundreds of Indian guides and slaves, priests, missionaries, horses, and great herds of cattle, pigs, and sheep. When Coronado and his entourage reached Cibola—actually the Zuni country of New Mexico—they found neither wealth nor splendor in the Indian pueblos.

Unsatisfied, Coronado and his party continued their search. They traveled through what later became the states of Arizona, New Mexico, Texas, Oklahoma, and Kansas. They saw the Continental Divide and claimed much of the Great Southwest for Spain. One group, on a side exploration, became the first white men to see the Grand Canyon.

Although Coronado found no cities of gold—no El Dorado—his expedition acquainted the Spanish with the Pueblo Indians and opened the American Southwest for settlement.

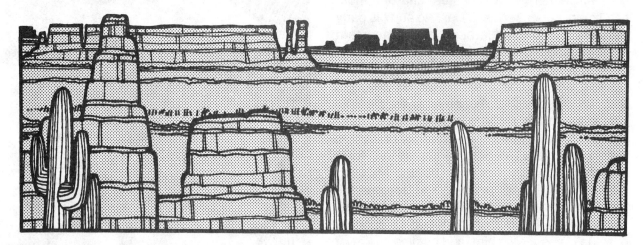

Activities

KN CO
1. Newell Convers Wyeth (1882–1945) was an American artist whose illustrations enlivened the pages in early editions of Robert Louis Stevenson's *Kidnapped* and *Treasure Island* and whose murals adorn walls in the Missouri State Capitol, the Federal Reserve Bank at Boston, and elsewhere. Find a picture of Wyeth's painting of Coronado. Study this picture, paying special attention to the clothing worn by Coronado and others in it.

KN CO
2. The Spanish words **El Dorado** literally mean "the gilded man." During the sixteenth century, El Dorado was the mythical country of the Golden Man sought by adventurers in South America. Do some research to learn about the legendary basis for this ancient idea and about how this term is used figuratively today.

AN SY EV
3. The Spaniards introduced horses, sheep, cattle, iron tools, and Christianity to the Indians of the South, Central, and North America. These European visitors also brought diseases, such as measles and smallpox, to which the Indians had never been exposed and against which they had no immunity. As a result, large numbers of Indians became ill and died. Analyze and evaluate the ways in which expeditions such as Coronado's affected the Indians of the American Southwest. In what ways was Indian contact with Europeans beneficial? In what ways was it harmful? Summarize your ideas in a brief written report. Include in this report some charts or graphs that illustrate the drastic effect that European weapons and diseases had on an unprepared Indian population.

Name _____

French Interest in the New World

France, too, was interested in the New World. Norman and Breton fishermen probably visited Newfoundland as early as 1500. Between 1534 and 1541, Jacques Cartier explored parts of what is now Canada, including the St. Lawrence River and the sites on which the cities of Quebec and Montreal now stand. Between 1603 and 1615, French explorer Samuel de Champlain accompanied fur-trading expeditions along the St. Lawrence River and explored the Great Lakes region from New York down to the lake that bears his name.

French explorers soon recognized that this part of the New World offered a treasure far different from the gold and jewels sought by the Spanish conquistadors in Central and South America. This treasure was the thick pelts of the animals that roamed the northern wilderness. These animals could be trapped and skinned; and when their fur was sold, it would bring a handsome profit.

As the fur trade increased, so did the need for a relatively simple way to ship pelts from the northern wilderness to southern ports and European markets. This need was met in 1682 when Robert Cavelier Sieur de La Salle descended the Mississippi River to the Gulf of Mexico and claimed the entire valley for Louis XIV, naming the region Louisiana in honor of this French monarch. The French could now use a vast network of lakes and rivers that extended from northeastern Canada to the Gulf of Mexico and included the Great Lakes and the St. Lawrence, Ohio, and Mississippi rivers to transport their precious cargo.

To control the fur trade, to prevent the British from occupying the lower Mississippi, and to provide themselves with a base from which to halt the Spanish advance, French forces founded a colony in Louisiana in 1699 and in 1718 founded the city of New Orleans at the mouth of the Mississippi. In this way, the French came to control all of the land from the Mississippi River west to the Rocky Mountains and from the port of New Orleans north into Canada.

Activities

KN CO 1. The text states that "Norman and Breton fishermen probably visited Newfoundland as early as 1500." Who were the **Normans**? Who were the **Bretons**? In what way was each one of these groups related to France?

KN CO 2. The English language as it is spoken today was enriched by the French influence during the period of exploration, discovery, and settlement. For example, from French came the words **bayou**, **bureau**, **cache**, **caribou**, **chowder**, **levee**, and **portage**. Look up each one of these words to learn how it is pronounced and what it means.

KN CO 3. From the Indians, English-speaking settlers borrowed a number of words naming Indian foods and having to do with the Indian way of life. These borrowed words include **canoe**, **hominy**, **mackinaw**, **moccasin**, **papoose**, **pone**, **squaw**, **succotash**, **tapioca**, **toboggan**, **tomahawk**, **wampum**, and **wigwam**. Look up each one of these words to learn how it is pronounced and what it means.

The Old World Divides the New

Once European monarchs became convinced of the existence of the New World, they sponsored expeditions to it for the purposes of increasing their wealth and extending their territory. For example, in 1497, Italian seafarer John Cabot, sailing west under the Union Jack, reached Newfoundland or Cape Breton Island and claimed much of the mainland of North America for England. In 1500, at the request of King Emanuel I of Portugal, Pedro Alvares Cabral set sail for the East Indies, was blown off course, and accidentally discovered Brazil. On Easter Sunday in 1513, Juan Ponce de León, the Spanish governor of Puerto Rico, discovered Florida while searching for the fabled fountain of youth; and twenty-three years later, Hernando de Soto, with the permission of Charles V of Spain, set out to conquer Florida and to explore the southeastern part of North America.

Between 1519 and 1521, Hernando Cortes decimated the Aztec Empire and established Spanish rule throughout Mexico. In 1540, Francisco Vásquez de Coronado, another Spanish explorer, wandered the southwestern part of North America in a futile search for El Dorado and established Spain's claim to that area. And in the early 1600s, Henry Hudson, an English navigator who sailed at different times for Dutch and English commercial interests, entered Hudson Strait and explored Hudson Bay in what is now northern Canada.

Thus, by the end of the seventeenth century, Old World nations had explored a large part of the New World and had divided it into well-defined spheres of influence. England claimed much of what became Canada. France controlled the North American heartland from the forests of Canada to the mouth of the mighty Mississippi. Spain claimed Florida and the southwestern part of what became the United States. Spain also claimed Mexico, Central America, and most of South America, with the exception of a relatively small area along the Spanish Main—which belonged to England, France, and Holland—and of Brazil, which belonged, by virtue of serendipity, to Portugal.

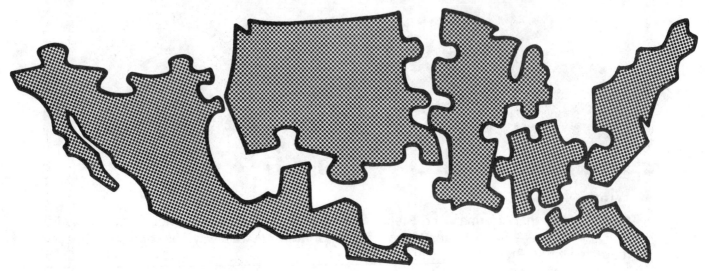

Activities

KN
CO
AP

1. On the map on page 71, use different colors to indicate the approximate location and extent of the Aztec Empire and of the Inca Empire (described on pages 63 and 66 of this book). Add these colors and what they stand for to the legend.

AN
SY

2. Compare the map on page 71 with some other map to discover the approximate scale that was used in drawing the former. How many miles does one inch equal? Add this information to the map legend also.

Name _____

The Old World Divides the New
(continued)

Legend

- England
- France
- Holland
- Portugal
- Spain

Name _____

Correlated Activities

KN
CO
AP
AN
SY
Create separate but parallel illustrated time lines detailing the exploration efforts sponsored by England, France, Holland, Portugal, and Spain between 1400 and 1600. Compare the discoveries made by these five countries during this period and the territories claimed by each one of them at the end of this period. Which country sponsored the most discoveries? Which country had laid claim to the most territory? List several ways in which these discoveries and claims led to international disputes and influenced the acquisition of language and the unfolding of history.

KN
CO
AP
One of the problems that early explorers faced was having to use maps that were both inaccurate and incomplete. Cartographers often had to do their work from memory, from notes hastily scribbled aboard a tossing ship, and sometimes even from hearsay. They were forced by circumstances to base much of their work on educated guesses rather than on careful measurement. To understand the difficulties faced by sixteenth-century mapmakers, pretend that you are a cartographer and that you must create a map from memory. Think of a particular place with which you are familiar—an amusement park, a camp, a city block, a farm, a national park or monument, or a recreation area. Without going back to this place, draw a map of it entirely *from memory*. Make your map as accurate and as detailed as possible. Label each important feature, and try to make the distances proportional. When you have finished drawing the map, add a legend in which you indicate the approximate scale to which your map is drawn and identify the symbols you have used to represent frequently occurring features.

When you go on a camping trip in a remote area, you must buy and carry with you all of the food and supplies you will need until you once again return to "civilization" with its food, clothing, and hardware stores. When the explorers set sail for the New World from European ports, they, too, had to carry all of the food and supplies they would need until they once again sailed into port. You are the quartermaster for one of the expeditions described in this unit. It is your job to purchase the food that will be needed to feed the crew throughout the planned voyage.

KN
CO
AP
First, determine how many crew members there will be and what amounts of meat, grain, vegetables, and fresh water each one will need daily.

KN
CO
AP
Second, use your knowledge of the distance between ports and the average speed of the ship in which you will be sailing to determine the number of days the journey will take.

KN
CO
AP
Third, on the basis of the amount of food needed daily and the number of days the trip is expected to take, determine what quantities of meat, grain, vegetables, and fresh water you will need for the entire voyage.

KN
CO
AP
AN
Fourth, do some research to determine what foods were available in sixteenth-century Europe and what methods could be used to preserve these foods for long periods aboard ship. For example, could foods be canned, dried, freeze dried, frozen, refrigerated, and/or salted? On the basis of this information, make a shopping list of the groceries you will need.

AN
SY
Fifth, if possible, find out the approximate cost of these grocery items and compare them with the approximate costs of similar quantities of comparable items today.

AP
AN
SY
Finally, calculate approximately how much all of these groceries will weigh at the start of the voyage and how much space will be needed to store them. Compare these weight and space figures with the total cargo and crew space available aboard ship and with the total tonnage of a typical sailing vessel used for exploration. What percentage of the available space and weight would your foodstuffs require?

Correlated Activities
(continued)

You are the curator of a national history museum. It is your job to organize an exhibit that will give museum visitors some understanding of the Inca.

KN CO Select and list the types of artifacts and objects you will include in the exhibit. Use encyclopedias, pertinent issues of *National Geographic*, and other similar materials to learn what types of artifacts and objects are available; but rely on your own ideas about what people would like to see in making your selections.

AP Choose a name for the exhibit and create a logogram or symbol for it.

AP Design a brochure, flier, or poster to interest people in coming to see the exhibit. Explain in a few words the purpose and content of the exhibit, when and where it will be on display, the price (if any) that will be charged for admission, and how interested groups can make arrangements to view it.

AP Create a program for the exhibit. In this program, provide an introduction in which you give museum visitors some background information about Inca history and culture. Also, picture and describe each of the artifacts and objects you have selected for inclusion in the exhibit and explain its use, meaning, or significance within the Inca culture.

AP Design T-shirts, tote bags, badges, bumper stickers, or other similar items for sale to exhibit visitors in the museum souvenir and gift shop.

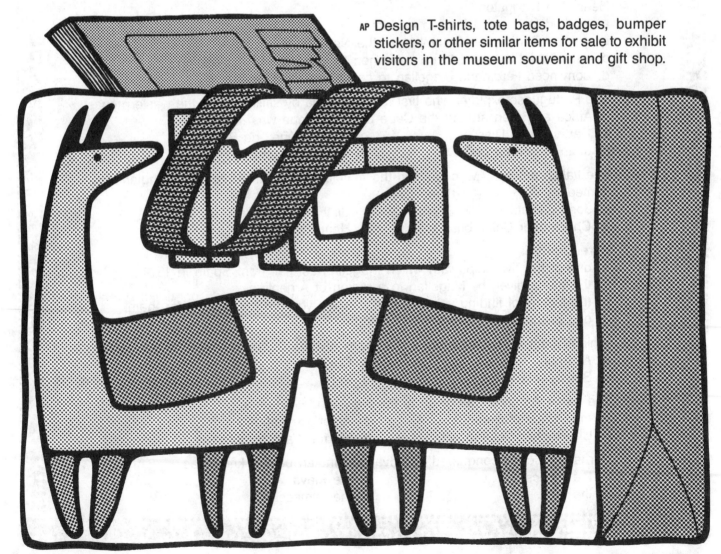

Name _____

Posttest

Circle the letter beside the best answer or the most appropriate response.

1. The Vikings were skilled shipbuilders and fearless navigators who
   a. never left Scandinavia.
   b. sailed only as far as France and England.
   c. led the way to the New World nearly five hundred years before Columbus.
   d. discovered the Cape of Good Hope.

2. Marco Polo did *not*
   a. journey to the Far East during the thirteenth century.
   b. travel by burro, camel, horseback, and ship.
   c. describe his amazing adventures to a fellow prisoner.
   d. discover Cathay.

3. A **cartographer**
   a. draws carts.   c. photographs cars.
   b. makes maps.   d. writes cards.

4. Henry the Navigator
   a. worked for several famous explorers.
   b. guided Christopher Columbus to the New World.
   c. established a school to train seamen for oceangoing exploration.
   d. convinced Ferdinand Magellan to continue sailing west.

5. The Portuguese explorer who first reached India by sailing down the western coast of Africa and then around the Cape of Good Hope was named
   a. Bartholomeu Dias.   c. Vasco Núñez de Balboa.
   b. Juan Ponce de León.   d. Vasco da Gama.

6. The Italian navigator who claimed the mainland of North America for England was named
   a. John Cabot.   c. Sir Francis Drake.
   b. Christopher Columbus.   d. Henry Hudson.

7. **Serendipity** is
   a. one of the five ships with which Magellan set sail from Spain in 1519.
   b. the name given by Magellan to a region of Argentina.
   c. the faculty of finding valuable things when you are not looking for them.
   d. one of the Spice Islands.

8. Which South American country did Pedro Alvares Cabral discover by accident?
   a. Argentina   c. Chile
   b. Brazil   d. Peru

9. The name America was given to the New World by
   a. the Prince of Serendip.   c. Amerigo Vespucci.
   b. Christopher Columbus.   d. Martin Waldseemüller.

10. Hernando Cortes conquered an advanced Indian people known as
    a. the Aztecs.   c. the Maya.
    b. the Inca.   d. the Olmecs.

Answer Key

Pretest, Page 40

1. c	6. a
2. a	7. a
3. c	8. b
4. c	9. a
5. c	10. c

Posttest, Page 74

1. c	6. a
2. d	7. c
3. b	8. b
4. c	9. d
5. d	10. a

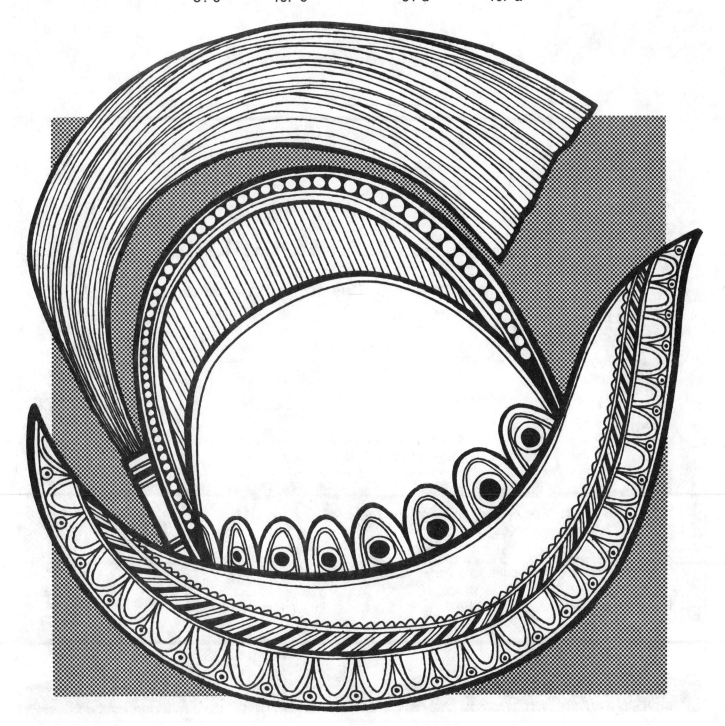

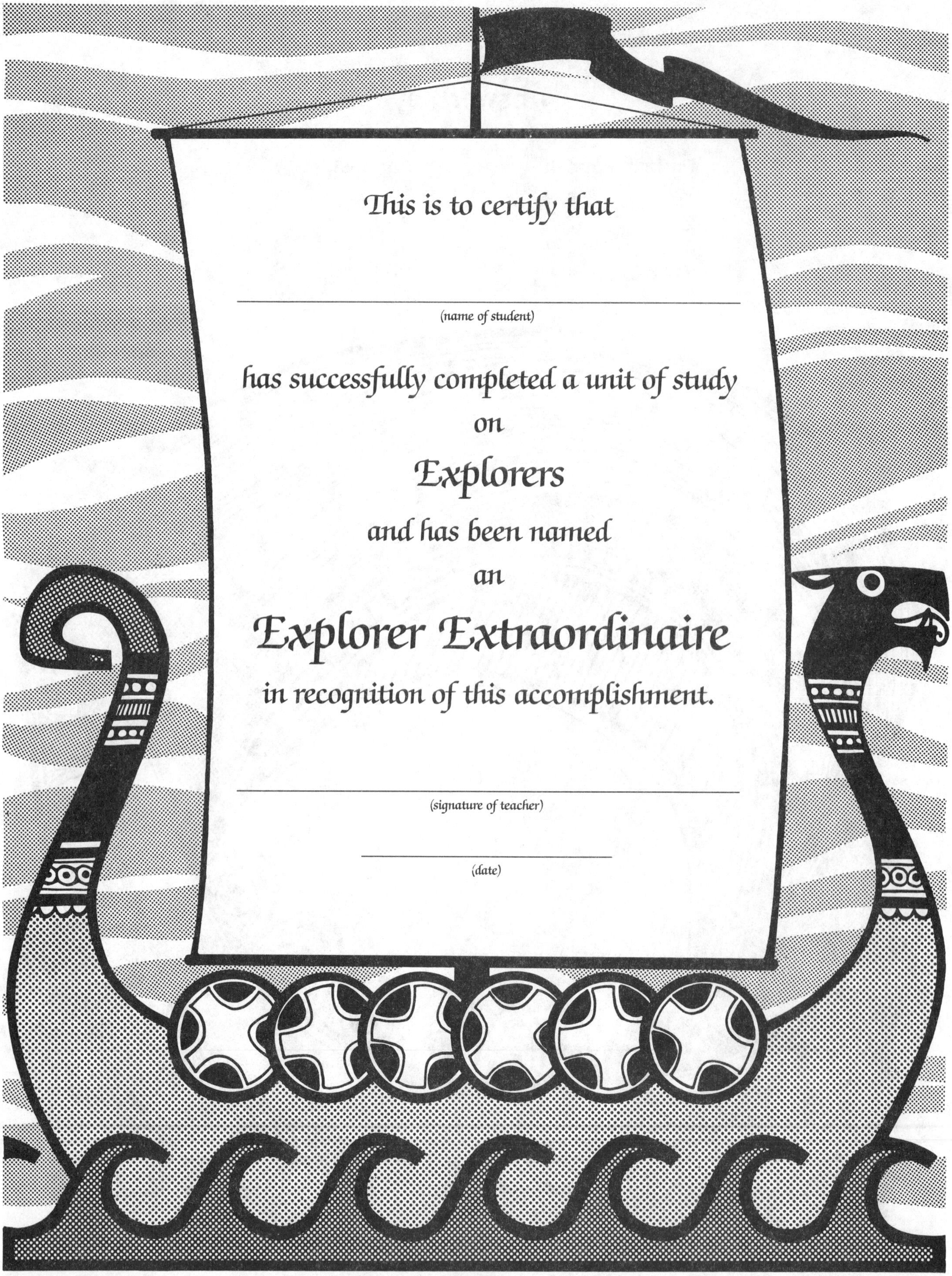

This is to certify that

_____

(name of student)

has successfully completed a unit of study
on
Explorers
and has been named
an
Explorer Extraordinaire
in recognition of this accomplishment.

_____

(signature of teacher)

_____

(date)

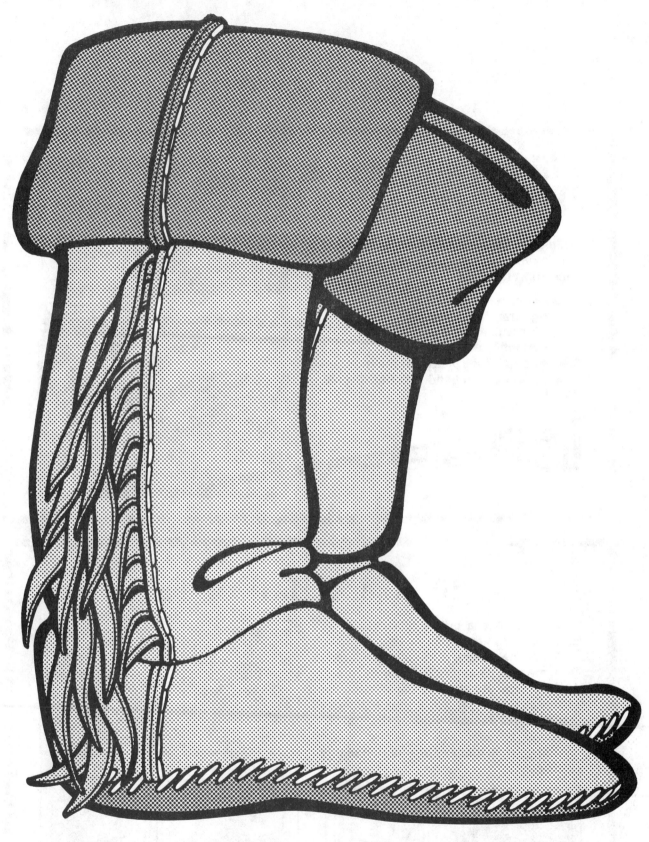

Trailblazers

Bulletin Board Ideas

Fill a Trailblazer's Backpack

Trailblazers usually traveled on foot and had to carry most of the things they needed in packs on their backs.

1. Do some research to learn what sorts of things trailblazers carried.
2. Decide which of these things was most important.
3. Draw and label a picture of the most important thing and add it to this display.

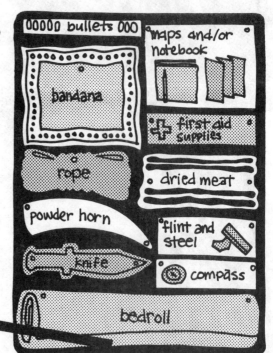

Trailblazers' Hall of Fame

1. Choose your favorite trailblazer.
2. Draw a picture of him or her.
3. Below the picture, write your trailblazer's name and dates of birth and death.
4. On a separate sheet of paper, describe the exploits that make your trailblazer worthy of membership in the Hall of Fame.
5. Add your picture and description to this display.

Learning Center Idea

Trailblazers' Techniques

Just like the trailblazers of a century or more ago, modern-day trailblazers need to know how to tell where they are and how to determine where they are going. At this center, you can familiarize yourself with some of the equipment and techniques used in this pathfinding process. For example, you can

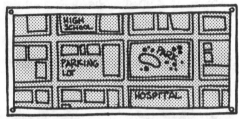

Neighborhood Map

- examine some of these types of maps
choropleth	road
isarithmic	topographic
relief	weather
- learn how a compass works
- learn how to read a map legend
- learn how to use a map scale to figure distance
- learn how to use letter and number coordinates to locate specific places or features on a map
- make a detailed map of the route you follow when you walk to school, to the store, or to a friend's house
- become familiar with the following terms

Topographic Map

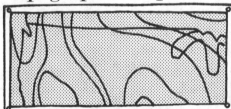

Isarithmic Map

altitude	index
atlas	latitude
chorography	legend
compass	longitude
compass rose	magnetic north
contour lines	meridians
coordinates	parallels
geography	projection
grid	rhumb line
elevation	symbols
topography	

compasses

Name _____

Pretest

Circle the letter beside the best answer or the most appropriate response.

1. The Cumberland Gap is
   a. an open space between two forests.
   b. a pass in the Sierra Nevada discovered by Joseph Cumberland.
   c. a natural passageway in the Appalachian Mountains.
   d. another name for the Continental Divide.

2. Who blazed a trail from Tennessee to Kentucky through the Appalachian Mountains?
   a. Daniel Boone
   b. Kit Carson
   c. Davy Crockett
   d. John Charles Frémont

3. Who captured three British forts with a small band of men and thereby strengthened the United States claim to the Northwest Territory?
   a. Moses Austin
   b. James Beckwourth
   c. George Rogers Clark
   d. William Clark

4. The Northwest Territory was later divided into which five states?
   a. Illinois, Indiana, Michigan, Ohio, and Wisconsin
   b. Iowa, Minnesota, North Dakota, South Dakota, and Wisconsin
   c. Montana, Nebraska, North Dakota, South Dakota, and Wyoming
   d. Idaho, Montana, Oregon, Washington, and Wyoming

5. Which territorial purchase was the largest piece of land ever sold at one time and possibly the best land bargain in history?
   a. Alaska
   b. the Gadsden Purchase
   c. the Louisiana Purchase
   d. Texas

6. The Lewis and Clark expedition was commissioned to explore
   a. the Gadsden Purchase.
   b. the Louisiana Purchase.
   c. the Northwest Territory.
   d. Oregon Territory.

7. Lewis and Clark began their journey with two pirogues. A **pirogue** is a type of
   a. boat.
   b. French hat.
   c. rifle.
   d. wagon.

8. Sacagawea was an energetic Indian maiden who aided the Lewis and Clark expedition. Her name means
   a. Adventurer.
   b. Bird Woman.
   c. Morning Star.
   d. Shy One.

9. Lone white adventurers who spent their time hunting and trapping in the Rockies or the Sierra Nevada were called
   a. mountain men.
   b. Nevada navigators.
   c. Nevada nomads.
   d. sons of the Sierra.

10. One of the first white women to cross the Continental Divide was
    a. Jane Addams.
    b. Rebecca Boone.
    c. Sacagawea.
    d. Narcissa Whitman.

Name _____

America's Shifting Frontier

At the moment colonists first settled on the eastern shores of America, a westward movement began that carried them across the continent. For more than two centuries, daring pioneers pushed the frontier farther and farther west. At first, these pioneers traveled on foot and horseback through the Cumberland Gap and by barge, raft, and steamboat down the Ohio and Mississippi rivers and up the Missouri. Later, they traveled by covered wagon, following the trails blazed by those who had gone on foot before them.

The westward movement of these pioneers was slowed by dense forests, raging waters, high mountains, desolate prairies, waterless deserts, wild animals, debilitating disease, Indian attack, and inclement weather; but they struggled onward, following their dream of a better life.

Westward expansion came in waves. The first frontier along the eastern seacoast was settled by 1763. Then pioneers moved across the Appalachian Mountains. After the War of 1812, they pushed west and south to settle the Mississippi Valley from the Gulf of Mexico to the Great Lakes. In the two decades before the Civil War, settlers moved as far west as California. During and after that war, they settled the Rocky Mountain and Great Plains regions.

Activities

KN
CO
AP

1. Familiarize yourself with the following terms: **adventurer, discoverer, discovery, expedition, experiment, exploration, explorer, frontier, guide, mountaineer, mountain man, pathfinder, pioneer, safari, scout, trader, trailblazer,** and **trapper.** Use these terms to start a **Discovery Dictionary.** Print each term on a separate sheet of paper. Beside each term, show in parentheses how it should be pronounced. Below the term, write its definition or description. Next, write a sentence in which you use the term. Then, on the bottom half of the sheet of paper, draw a picture that would help you explain this term to someone who has never heard it before. Finally, below the picture or on a separate sheet of paper, write some words, names, or ideas that come to mind when you hear or read this term. For example, the term **expedition** might make you think of **Marco Polo,** or the term **frontier** might make you think of the **ocean floor** or of **space.** Punch holes down the left-hand side of each one of these sheets and tie them together with yarn or place them in a three-ring binder. Expand your dictionary by adding new pages as you encounter other related terms and ideas.

KN
CO
AP

2. The westward migration of settlers often had devastating effects on the wildlife and on the Indians who inhabited the land. Write a poem, paragraph, essay, play, or short story in which you depict westward expansion from the point of view of an animal or a person who has been displaced or dispossessed.

AN
SY

3. Each new wave of people going west built upon and profitted from the experiences of those who had gone before. Each group learned or left behind something that made it easier for the next group to survive or succeed. In some ways, life is a trailblazing experience, an adventure in a place you have never been before. In what ways can those who have gone before you help you find your way? In what ways can you help those who come after you? List some of these ways. Then compare your list with one created by a friend.

A Predictable Procession of Pioneers

A predictable procession of pioneers moved forward with each wave of westward expansion. First came explorers, fur trappers, and traders. These adventurers made no attempt to settle in the wilderness. Instead, they simply passed through, following trails blazed earlier by herds of deer and buffalo, and by the Indians who tracked these animals. After the trappers and hunters came soldiers, miners, and cattlemen. Members of these groups explored and prepared the way, but never really tamed their surroundings.

Then came the pioneer farmers, who cleared patches of land and built rough log cabins but moved on when their neighbors got too close or their own wanderlust became too strong. After the pioneer farmers came another group of farmers, the first real settlers in the west. These men brought their families and sank their roots deep into the frontier soil. They not only cleared land and built cabins but also erected fences and graded roads. Last came the doctors, lawyers, merchants, and others who provided necessary services to growing pioneer communities. This predictable procession of pioneers pushed America's settled boundaries toward the Pacific Ocean.

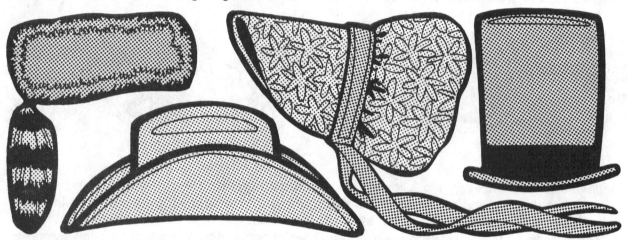

Activities

CO
AP
AN

1. Before wagons could make the trip west, a traveler had to carry in a pack on his back all of the supplies he might need during his journey. Do some research to discover what items frontiersmen carried to help them cope with life in the wilderness. On a large sheet of paper or a piece of poster board, list some of these items, draw a picture of each one, and briefly describe its use or purpose.

CO
AP
AN
SY
EV

2. Pretend that you are a modern-day scout or guide and that you are preparing for a two-week trip into the wilderness. Your supplies will be limited to what you are able to carry. Make a list of the items you plan to take. Beside each item, explain how you will use it to obtain food or water, or to sustain and protect yourself. As you choose these items, consider their weight, their bulk, and their usefulness. For example, is there one item that might do the work of two or three others? Can all of these items fit in a backpack? And if they can fit, will you be able to carry the pack as you walk?

SY
EV

3. Compare the list you made in activity 1 with the list you made in activity 2. In what ways are these lists similar? In what ways are they different? What factors might account for these similarities and differences? Have basic human needs changed in the past two hundred years? Have recent discoveries and inventions changed the ways in which these needs are met today? Are all of these discoveries and inventions applicable to a wilderness situation? Why or why not?

Name _____

Daniel Boone (1734–1820)

Even before the Revolutionary War, pioneers were pushing the American frontier westward from the Atlantic Coast. Daniel Boone was one of these pioneers. He grew up on the advancing frontier and blazed a trail so others could settle there.

Daniel Boone was born in a log cabin on the Pennsylvania frontier in 1734. Boone's parents were hardworking Quakers who had a small farm, a blacksmith shop, and a weaving establishment. Young Daniel shared the household and farm chores with the other children in the Boone family. When he was not tending the cows, he learned woodcraft from friendly Indians and hunted with his rifle in the surrounding wilderness.

When Daniel was seventeen, his father felt crowded by the large number of more recent settlers and decided to move his family to the wild frontier along the Yadkin River in North Carolina. In this new setting, Daniel used his well-developed hunting skills to provide meat for the family. He traded the animal skins for lead, powder, salt, and other necessities that the Boones could not grow or make.

As a result of various expeditions, both England and France claimed substantial portions of North America. Their struggle for empire found expression in the so-called French and Indian Wars, which took place between 1689 and 1754 and between 1755 and 1763. These wars were fought to determine whether France or England would have the opportunity to settle and exploit the American West.

In these wars, the English fought both the French and the Indians for possession of key forts and control of claimed territories. When the British were ultimately victorious, England gained control of Canada and of all French possessions east of the Mississippi River except the New Orleans region. As a result, pioneers from the English colonies along the Atlantic coast regarded this area as being officially open for settlement.

Daniel Boone drove a supply wagon during the second French and Indian War. From other settlers, he heard stories about a land called Kentucky, on the other side of the Appalachian Mountains, where the buffalo grew fat, the deer roamed free, and there were so many wild turkeys that they could not all fly at once. Determined to blaze a trail into this hunter's paradise, Boone worked with a group of axmen to clear a road from the Holston River in Tennessee to the Kentucky River in Kentucky through the Cumberland Gap, a natural passage in the Appalachian Mountains, where the present states of Virginia, Kentucky, and Tennessee meet. Over this trail, which became known as Wilderness Road, Boone led his family and other pioneers into the wilderness he felt "ordained of God to settle." Together in 1775, these pioneers built a fort and established a settlement called Boonesboro in the Kentucky wilderness, near the site of present-day Lexington. Boone's wife Rebecca and his daughter Jemima were the first white women to see this part of Kentucky.

Daniel Boone (1734–1820)
(continued)

Boone's hunting and trailblazing frequently took him into the back country, where he encountered both friendly and unfriendly Indians. Captured several times, he used his cunning to escape. In fact, Blackfish, a Shawnee chief, had so much respect for Boone that the Indian adopted him into the Shawnee tribe.

As more and more pioneers moved into Kentucky and more and more land was needed to house them, Boone expressed a willingness to sell the land he had claimed, but lawyers informed him that he had failed to register his claim to the land and to get title. For this reason, they said, he had no legal right to it. As a result, Boone lost all of his land in Kentucky.

In search of new territory, Boone moved to Point Pleasant in what is now West Virginia. Later, because he needed "more elbow room," he settled on land used by the Femme Osage Indians in Missouri, where Spanish officials made him magistrate. But when this territory came under control of the United States government, Boone once again lost his land because he had registered his claim with the Spanish, whose laws had been declared invalid when the United States gained possession of this area. Not until 1814 did the United States Congress return to Boone some of the land he had claimed, in recognition of his having "opened the way for millions of his fellow men."

Daniel Boone spent his last years in Missouri, hunting whenever he could, and died there at the age of eighty-six. Today, the trail he blazed from his early family home on the Yadkin River in North Carolina to Boonesboro, Kentucky, is marked in his honor.

Activities

KN
CO

1. The text states that Daniel Boone's family were "hardworking Quakers." Find out more about the **Quakers**. Who were they? Where did they come from? Where did they settle? What did they believe? By what other names are they known? Which other famous Americans have been Quakers? Share what you learn with the class.

KN
CO
AP
AN

2. On a detailed map of the United States, trace the route Daniel Boone might have followed from his birthplace near Reading, Pennsylvania; south through Maryland and Virginia to the Yadkin River in North Carolina; west into Tennessee; northwest from the Holston River in Tennessee to the Kentucky River in Kentucky through the Cumberland Gap (at the point where the present-day states of Virginia, Kentucky, and Tennessee meet); then north and slightly west to the Boonesboro site near what is now Lexington, Kentucky. Using the scale given on the map, estimate the total distance Daniel Boone and the pioneers who followed him traveled. Take special note of the natural and geographic features that would have been an impedence to travel by foot or wagon. List some of these features.

AN
SY
EV

3. Who owns the land? The Indians, who were the first inhabitants of North America, believed that the land—like the clean air and clear water—belonged to everyone and to no one. It was meant to be roamed rather than fenced and cared for but not claimed. The English, the French, and the Spanish, who "discovered" and explored the land, claimed portions of it as parts of their empires. Frontiersman Daniel Boone claimed parts of Kentucky because he had blazed a trail to it, explored it, and settled on it. The settlers Boone led west over Wilderness Road claimed as their own the land they cleared and farmed. And the United States government asserted its jurisdiction over territories that came under its control as a result of treaty or purchase. Frequently, these claims overlapped, and conflicts arose. Divide your class or group so that students represent the Indians, the English, the French, and the Spanish, Daniel Boone and other frontiersmen, a group of pioneer settlers, and the United States government. Do some research and then present the land claims of each group. After the presentation, evaluate the legitimacy of these claims to answer the question: Who owns the land?

George Rogers Clark (1752–1818)

"If a country is not worth protecting, it is not worth claiming," declared George Rogers Clark. The time was the Revolutionary War. The place was the Virginia Council. Clark was pleading with council members to send gunpowder to settlers in Kentucky, which was then a Virginia county, so that they would be prepared to defend themselves against British and Indian attack. Clark knew that England hoped to destroy the Kentucky forts and control all of the region west of the Allegheny Mountains, including the rich Ohio River Valley.

George Rogers Clark was born on November 19, 1752, near Charlottesville, Virginia. As a young man, he worked as a surveyor in the Kentucky wilderness, where he measured off land to be sold to settlers. His travels took him to all of the forts in Kentucky. In time, he became a spokesman for these forts and then commander of Kentucky's militia. He understood the strategic value of the Kentucky forts and the importance of the Ohio River Valley.

The Ohio River Valley had originally been claimed by the French, but they had lost this valley to England in the French and Indian War. To protect their claim, the British had built several forts. In addition, they had begun supplying the Indians with arms and encouraging them to make raids on the pioneers as a way of discouraging further non-British settlement in the area.

Clark wanted the pioneers to be prepared to defend themselves, but he was not content with mere defense. Instead, he devised a plan to capture the British forts and settle the matter once and for all by winning the territory for the American colonists. Clark gained the approval of Patrick Henry, governor of Virginia, for an expedition to conquer Illinois country, which was also known as the Northwest Territory. Henry's approval did not carry with it an appropriation of funds, so Clark used his own money to hire a small band of soldiers.

In May 1778, Clark and his band sailed down the Ohio River from Louisville, Kentucky. After abandoning their boats near the point at which the Ohio flows into the Mississippi, they crept overland through the Illinois forest to the British fort at Kaskaskia. On July 4, 1778, Clark and his soldiers surprised the Redcoats and took the fort. The British fort at Cahokia, near present-day St. Louis, surrendered a few days later. Clark and his small band of men had taken both British strongholds without firing a single shot.

George Rogers Clark (1752–1818)
(continued)

Not pleased with this turn of events, the British decided to recapture both forts. With this purpose in mind, Colonel Henry Hamilton and his Redcoats wintered at Vincennes in southwestern Indiana, thinking that they would return to Illinois in the spring and retake the two forts. Instead, Clark and his small band of men marched more than two hundred miles through dense forests and icy swamps to surprise Hamilton and take Vincennes in late February 1779.

With this victory, the British stranglehold on the Ohio Valley was broken. Clark's successful campaign had secured for America all of the Northwest Territory, which later became the states of Illinois, Indiana, Michigan, Ohio, and Wisconsin.

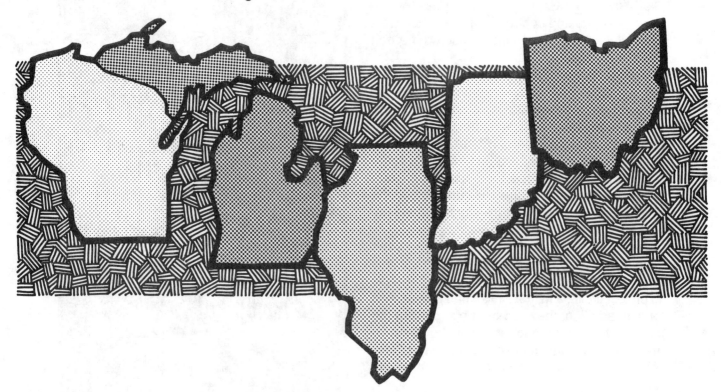

Activities

KN CO 1. Look at a map of North America. Note the present-day boundary between Canada and the United States. Recall that the British retained control of Canada but lost control of the Ohio River Valley as a result of George Rogers Clark's exploits. Consider where the United States-Canadian border might be today if Clark had been unsuccessful. Under these circumstances, which five states might lie north of the border and be a part of Canada?

KN CO 2. In the attack on Vincennes, Clark outwitted an army that was more than three times larger than his own little band. Find and read an account of Clark's capture of this British stronghold. What tricks did this American frontier leader use to outwit his enemies?

AN SY EV 3. In truth, Clark funded the salaries and supplies for his band of soldiers out of his own pocket. As a result, he was left nearly penniless. Do some research to learn why the Virginia government was unwilling to support Clark's campaign. Present your findings during a staged debate in which one student plays the role of Clark and argues in favor of funding and other students play the roles of Patrick Henry and Virginia Council members, some of whom favor funding and some of whom oppose it.

Name _____

The Best Land Bargain in History

In 1801, when Thomas Jefferson was inaugurated as the third president of the United States, this country owned only the land between the Atlantic Ocean and the Mississippi River. The vast area from the Mississipi River west to the Rocky Mountains was known as the Louisiana Territory and belonged to France.

As the population of the United States grew, hundreds of families moved across the Appalachian Mountains in search of free farmland. They cleared the forests and planted crops. These industrious pioneer farmers raised more produce and livestock than they could use, but selling what they did not need was difficult. It was too hard to haul loads back and forth over the mountains because there were no smooth roads, only narrow, rutted trails, which seasonal rains turned into muddy morasses.

The easiest way for these farmers to transport their goods was by boat down the Ohio River to the Mississippi and then down the Mississippi River to the port of New Orleans on the Gulf of Mexico. From there, oceangoing vessels could take them to ports along the eastern seaboard or even to Europe.

But the port of New Orleans did not belong to the United States. At this time, it was controlled by France. United States leaders feared that Napoleon Bonaparte, who was then the ruler of France, might decide to prevent Americans from using this port. If the Emperor did as they feared, many American farmers would have no way to transport their goods to market.

One way to prevent Napoleon from closing New Orleans to American shipping was to buy this port from him. In 1803, President Jefferson

The Best Land Bargain in History
(continued)

sent James Monroe to France as minister extraordinary to ask Napoleon if the United States could buy New Orleans and West Florida from France for the sum of $10 million. Napoleon surprised Monroe by offering to sell not only New Orleans but the entire Louisiana Territory for $15 million. When Monroe told Jefferson, the President instructed Monroe to accept the French offer.

The Louisiana Purchase, as this territory came be be called, measured nearly 828,000 square miles and was the largest piece of land ever sold at one time. Its acquisition almost doubled the size of the United States, which stretched, after its addition, from the Atlantic Ocean to the Rocky Mountains. Hailed as the best land bargain in history, this new territory had thousands of acres of fertile farm and grazing land. Vast mineral resources lay beneath its surface, waiting to be mined. And from its acreage was carved part or all of fifteen separate states.

Activities

KN CO AP

1. During the seventy years between 1800 and 1870, the United States nearly tripled its total size by means of purchase, cession, and treaty. First, do some research to learn about U.S. territorial expansion by means of these three methods. Then, create a time line or a map on which you show how, when, and from whom the United States acquired the land that now lies within its borders.

KN CO AP

2. Thomas Jefferson did not go to France to negotiate directly with Napoleon Bonaparte for the purchase of the Louisiana Territory. Instead, he remained in the United States and sent James Monroe to France as minister extraordinary and gave him the authority to offer as much as $10 million if necessary to purchase the Isle of Orleans and West Florida. Once Monroe arrived, a bargain was quickly struck whereby the United States would pay $5 million more to purchase the entire Louisiana Territory; however, West Florida was not included in the deal because France had not acquired title to it. Because of British supremacy on the seas, the French believed that they had little hope of holding onto this faraway piece of property and that their territorial interests would be better served by selling it and using the money they obtained in this way to finance their war against Great Britain. First, do some research to learn more about the circumstances surrounding the sale and purchase of the Louisiana Territory. Then, write a short play in which Napoleon Bonaparte, Thomas Jefferson, Robert R. Livingston, James Monroe, and Charles Maurice de Tallyrand-Perigord decide the fate of this large and valuable piece of property.

The Lewis and Clark Expedition

Although the Louisiana Purchase was hailed as the best land bargain in history, no one was certain exactly what the United States had acquired. Most of the land was unknown except to the Indians who inhabited it. To answer questions about the acquisition, President Thomas Jefferson commissioned Meriwether Lewis to explore it. He was to ascend the Missouri River to its source, to cross over the Continental Divide, and then to descend the Columbia River to its mouth.

Meriwether Lewis, an American explorer who was born in Albermarle County, Virginia, in 1774, was serving as private secretary to Jefferson when the President asked him to lead the expedition to explore the Louisiana Purchase. Lewis, in turn, chose William Clark as his co-leader. A younger brother of Revolutionary frontier leader George Rogers Clark, William Clark was a soldier who had been engaged for five years in frontier service against Indians.

The primary goal of the Lewis and Clark expedition was to survey for a practical land-water route to the Pacific Ocean for the purposes of preparing the way for commercial exchange with the Indians, establishing a lucrative fur trade, and opening the American West for settlement. Lewis and Clark were instructed to keep extensive records of the wildlife, mineral resources, geographic features, and climatic conditions they observed and to determine the tribal affiliations of the Indians they encountered. Their journals became the basis for a book published in 1814 under the self-explanatory but somewhat cumbersome title *History of the Expedition Under the Commands of Captains Lewis and Clark*.

In the fall of 1803, Lewis and Clark went to St. Louis, Missouri, set up camp for the winter, and began training the men who would accompany them on their journey. The following spring, Lewis received for his government the formal transfer of the upper part of Louisiana from France to the United States. On May 14, 1804, Lewis and Clark started up the Missouri River with three boats—one fifty-five-foot keelboat and two pirogues. These boats could be rowed, poled, paddled, or sailed by men on board, or they could be towed with long ropes by men on shore. The vessels were loaded with six tons of food, ammunition, medical supplies, and trinkets for trading with the Indians.

More than forty men accompanied Lewis and Clark on the first leg of the their trip. Most of them were soldiers or backwoodsmen who had been handpicked by the expedition leaders. Even after extensive training, however, these seasoned veterans were unprepared for the arduous journey that lay ahead. They would have no contact with home for more than two years and would face hardships and obstacles that none of them could foresee at the outset. Among these obstacles was the need to row upstream against a much stiffer current than anyone had anticipated.

By the fall of 1804, Lewis, Clark, and their men had reached Mandan Indian villages more than one thousand miles upriver, north of what is now Bismarck, North Dakota, near Washburn. Here they built a strong three-sided fort and some huts in which they could spend the winter. While wintering among the Mandans, Lewis and Clark tried to learn as much as possible about the terrain that lay ahead.

The Lewis and Clark Expedition
(continued)

As luck would have it, a French Canadian fur trader named Toussaint Charbonneau was living in the Mandan village at this time. Always eager for money, Charbonneau offered to act as a guide and interpreter for Lewis and Clark on the remainder of their westward journey. Although the expedition leaders quickly realized that Charbonneau was a braggart who did not possess the expertise he claimed to have, they accepted the French Canadian's offer because he was married to Sacagawea. This young Shoshone Indian girl had grown up in the shadows of the Rocky Mountains and knew much about the land into which they were headed and about the Indians who inhabited this region.

In early April, Lewis and Clark broke camp. With the two pirogues and six canoes, they and thirty-one other adventurers, including Charbonneau, Sacagawea, and her baby, resumed the journey up the Missouri River. They had sent the keelboat back to St. Louis full of interesting plant and animal specimens and Indian trinkets for President Jefferson.

In May, Lewis, Clark, and their party reached the Great Falls of the Missouri in what is now Montana. Boats were of no use to them amid the rocks and churning rapids, so they built carts on which to haul their boats and supplies over land. The trek was so difficult that it took them nearly a month to travel the sixteen miles around the falls.

In what is now western Montana, Lewis and Clark had the good fortune of meeting up with Sacagawea's own tribe. Sacagawea's brother Cameahwait, who had become the chief, had not seen his sister since she had been kidnapped by the Minatarees, an enemy tribe, many years before. The Shoshones provided Lewis and Clark with horses and helped them through Lolo Pass on what is now the Montana-Idaho border. Following the narrow, rocky trails was more difficult than any other part of the trip. There was little food, and many of the men were cold, wet, and sick.

When Lewis and Clark reached what is now called the Clark Fork, they left their horses with friendly Indians, built canoes, and again entered the water, this time going downstream. They followed the Clark Fork to the Snake River, the Snake to the Columbia River, and the Columbia to where it empties into the Pacific Ocean at what is now Astoria, Washington. Because it was November, the exhausted explorers set up winter camp to provide some measure of shelter against the unceasing rains. Actually, they hoped to attract the attention of a trading ship sailing near the coast and to return east by boat rather than overland, but they were unsuccessful in their efforts.

In the spring of 1806, Lewis, Clark, and their party began the return trip overland. For a time, they split into two groups in the hope of finding a shorter route through the mountains. Both groups were reunited on the Missouri River, where they found downstream travel much faster than upstream travel.

The Lewis and Clark Expedition
(continued)

In September 1806, more than two years after Lewis and Clark had begun their journey, they returned to St. Louis. The townsfolk who had wished them good luck and Godspeed when they departed had long since given up hope of ever seeing them alive again and were astonished at their safe return.

Lewis and Clark had traveled more than eight thousand miles. They had seen things that no white man had ever seen. They had encountered grizzly bears, rattlesnakes, insects of all kinds, and unfriendly Indians. They had also seen great herds of buffalo on the plains and the "mighty shining mountains" of the West. As specimens, they had brought back plants, seeds, and live animals, as well as animal skins and skeletons. They also brought back maps and journals—all of which proved invaluable to the explorers and adventurers who followed in their footsteps.

The Lewis and Clark expedition showed the nation exactly what kind of bargain it had gotten with the purchase of Louisiana. It strengthened United States claims to Oregon Territory, stimulated the fur trade, and provided valuable scientific information about the American West.

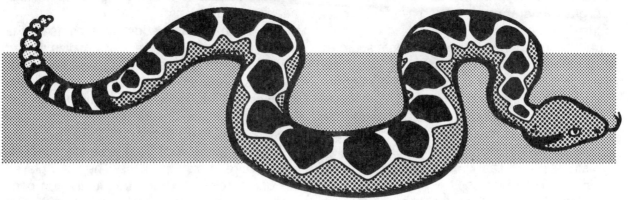

Activities

KN CO
1. Using the description in the text, trace the route Lewis and Clark followed from St. Louis, Missouri, to Astoria, Washington.

KN CO AP AN
2. The text says that Lewis and Clark "handpicked" the soldiers and backwoodsmen who went with them on their expedition. What qualities and skills would they have been looking for in the men they recruited to accompany them? Design an advertisement, circular, or poster in which you describe the position being offered and the qualities and skills that are wanted.

KN CO AP
3. According to the text, Lewis and Clark started their expedition with one **keelboat** and two **pirogues**. First, look up the names of each of these boats in a dictionary or encyclopedia to discover where these names came from, what these boats looked like, how they were propelled, what they were used for, and what their advantages and disadvantages were. Then, use this information to create a picture, poster, or chart.

AN SY EV
4. Compare a pirogue with a canoe. In what ways are these two boats similar? In what ways are they different? What are the advantages and disadvantages of each?

KN CO AP AN SY
5. Along the banks of the Upper Missouri, there was plenty of game, and members of the Lewis and Clark expedition ate well; but in the Rocky Mountains, as they ascended to Lolo Pass, food was scarce, and many of the men were "cold, wet, and sick." Do some reading to learn more about these two regions. Then, compare them. In what ways are they similar? In what ways are they different? What factors account for these differences? In answering this latter question, consider how weather conditions may vary with elevation and how plant and animal populations are affected by changes in climate, terrain, and weather.

Sacagawea (ca. 1787–1812)

Sacagawea was a Shoshone Indian born about 1787 in the rugged, mountainous territory where the present-day states of Idaho and Montana meet. The Shoshones were hunters and horse traders. During the late spring and summer, they lived in the high country, where they caught the salmon and other fish that swam in the swift-running mountain streams and carefully picked the plump, sweet berries that grew on the thorn-covered bushes. In the fall and winter, when the streams froze and snow blanketed the mountain meadows, the Shoshones moved down to warmer valleys, where their horses could still find grass for grazing and their braves could hunt buffalo and other wild game.

At the close of Sacagawea's eleventh summer, as the Shoshones were moving east, toward the place that is now called the Three Forks of the Missouri River, they encountered the Minatarees. These Indians raided the Shoshone camp, killing many braves and capturing Sacagawea and other Shoshone children. After the raid, the Minatarees rode east toward their own village, taking their hapless captives with them.

In the Minataree village, Sacagawea's life was very different from what it had been with the Shoshones. The Minatarees were farmers. They did not roam with the seasons, as the Shoshones had done, but stayed in one place so that they could plant, cultivate, and harvest. From them

Sacagawea learned how to plant and harvest corn, how to grind the kernels into meal, how to use this meal to make a coarse flour, how to form the moistened flour into loaves, and how to bake these loaves into bread.

The Minatarees were not only farmers but also hunters and trappers. In the forests and fields near their village, they hunted bear and buffalo and trapped bobcats, rabbits, and raccoons. When the Minataree hunters were successful, they had more pelts than they needed for clothing and ornaments. The surplus they gave to white traders in exchange for guns, bullets, beads, and blankets.

One of the white traders who came to the Minataree village was a French Canadian named Toussaint Charbonneau. Sacagawea had never seen a white man before. She could not help staring as Charbonneau bargained with the Minataree braves in sign language, and the French Canadian noticed her gaze.

Charbonneau loved to gamble, and the Indians were aware of his weakness. They had played his game before and had frequently won back from him the furs they had given in trade. But this time Charbonneau struck a different bargain. He did not want furs. Instead, he wanted the Indian maiden who stared at him. And this time, Charbonneau was lucky. In a game with Sacagawea's master, he won the girl.

Sacagawea (*ca.* 1787–1812)
(continued)

The next day Charbonneau and Sacagawea left the Minataree village. They traveled eastward for many days until they came to a place near what is now Bismarck, North Dakota, where some Mandan Indians lived. Charbonneau made his home among these Indians when he was not trading with tribes to the west. And it was the Mandans who first called the captured Shoshone maiden "Sacagawea." In their language, this name meant "Bird Woman." The Mandans gave it to Sacagawea because she was always flitting from place to place and reminded them of a small bird.

For Sacagawea, life among the Mandans was different from life with either the Shoshones or the Minatarees. Like the Minatarees, the Mandans lived in one place on the plains. They did not move about in the high country as the Shoshones had done. With the Mandan women, Sacagawea cured buffalo hides, sewed deerskin moccasins, planted corn, cooked meals, and dug the roots that were used for medicine.

When Sacagawea was about sixteen, her life changed again. In that year, Meriwether Lewis and William Clark wintered near the Mandan village. To the curious Indians, Lewis and Clark explained that they were leading a group of explorers and had just completed the first leg of a long journey across the American continent from St. Louis, Missouri, to the Pacific Ocean. Frequently, these two men asked the Indians questions about the unknown territory that lay ahead.

From the Indians, Charbonneau learned of the project Lewis and Clark were undertaking. Always eager for money, he offered to serve as their guide and interpreter for the remainder of their journey. In truth, Charbonneau was neither a qualified guide nor a skilled interpreter. Although he had traveled west and traded with Indians there, his ability to communicate with them was limited to the few words and signs needed to negotiate his trades. Lewis and Clark were aware that Charbonneau had misrepresented himself, but they accepted his offer on the condition that he bring Sacagawea with him.

When Charbonneau agreed, Sacagawea immediately began preparing for the journey. She mended tunics and made moccasins for the men to wear, she dried corn and smoked meat so they would have food to eat, and she fashioned a cradleboard for Jean Baptiste, her baby, who had been born in February. In April, when Lewis and Clark broke camp and left the Mandan village, Sacagawea bound her baby to the cradleboard. Then she, Charbonneau, and the baby—whom Lewis nicknamed Pomp—accompanied the explorers on the way west.

Sacagawea proved to be an invaluable asset to the expedition. The diverse skills she had learned from the different Indian tribes with which she had lived served her well, and several times her quick thinking and calm courage saved the men or their supplies from sudden and certain disaster.

Sacagawea (*ca.* 1787–1812)
(continued)

When the adventurers reached the high country beyond the Great Falls of the Missouri, they encountered the Shoshones, Sacagawea's people. William Clark noted in his journal that Sacagawea "showed every mark of extravagant joy" on seeing members of her own tribe once again, after so many years.

During Sacagawea's absence, her brother Cameahwait had grown up and had been made chief. Knowing how difficult the journey over the mountains was going to be for the explorers, Sacagawea asked her brother to help them. At first Cameahwait agreed, saying that he and his braves would act as guides and would help the white men carry their food and supplies. But later, when Cameahwait heard that buffalo were plen-tiful on the nearby plains, he decided to go east to hunt rather than going west with the expedition.

Sacagawea learned of her brother's abrupt change in plans. Fearing the white men would perish if their Indian guides deserted them, Sacagawea warned Lewis. In doing so, she betrayed her brother and became an outcast among her own people. When Lewis confronted Cameahwait, the Indian chief agreed to postpone the hunt and to keep his original promise to see the explorers safely over the Rocky Mountains. Thus, because of a young Indian girl named Sacagawea, Lewis and Clark were able to fulfill their commission and to find a route across the American continent to the Pacific Ocean.

Activities

KN CO AP 1. The fourth Friday in September is American Indian Day. Invite an Indian or someone knowledgeable about Indians to be your classroom guest on this day or to suggest ways in which you and your classmates might celebrate it.

KN CO 2. Sacagawea was a Shoshone. The Shoshones were a group of Indian peoples who spoke a language in the Shoshonean family and who inhabited an area that covers parts of the present states of California, Colorado, Idaho, Nevada, Utah, and Wyoming. At one time, Indian tribes were scattered throughout the United States. Find out something about the tribe or tribes that live or lived in your state or geographic area.

KN CO AP AN 3. The English language has been enriched by words borrowed from other languages. Among these words are Indian names given to places and geographic features. On a large map of the United States, locate some towns, states, and rivers that have Indian names. List twenty of them. Beside each one, describe what it is and where it is located.

AN SY 4. Sacagawea's experiences among the Shoshones, Minatarees, and Mandans were very different because all Indian tribes are *not* alike. Compare the customs and cultures of plains Indians with those of Indians living along the coasts, in the northern woodlands, or in the deep South. In what ways were they similar? In what ways were they different? Did they move about or stay put? What food did they eat and how did they obtain it? Were they farmers, gatherers, hunters, or trappers? What shelters did they build? What clothes did they wear and how did they make them? What tools did they use? Did they make pottery or weave baskets or blankets? What did they do for fun? Share what you learn by means of a chart or table on which you list such words as **food**, **clothing**, **shelter**, **tools**, and **fun** down the left-hand side; use the names of the tribes as column headings; and make appropriate custom and culture entries under each tribal name.

Zebulon Pike (1779–1813)

"At two o'clock in the afternoon I thought I could distinguish a mountain to our right, which appeared like a small blue cloud. Viewed it with the spy glass and was still more confirmed in my conjecture, . . ." This journal entry, dated Saturday, November 15, was written by Zebulon Pike in 1806, and records his discovery of the magnificent mountain that now bears his name.

Zebulon Montgomery Pike was born in Lamberton, New Jersey, in 1779. Twenty years later, he was commissioned as a first lieutenant in the U.S. Army. As a military officer, Pike was several times asked to lead small parties of soldiers on explorational missions. For example,

in 1805–1806, he and a small band made their way from St. Louis, Missouri, up the Mississippi River to its headwaters.

During the next year, while Lewis and Clark were returning from their trek across the American continent to the Pacific Ocean, Pike and his party set out to explore the southwestern part of the Louisiana Purchase. They left St. Louis on July 15, 1806, and traveled west, following the route of the Arkansas River during much of their journey. After four months, Pike spotted and described a distinctive mountain he called "Grand Peak." In his journal, he wrote that its summit was "entirely bare of vegetation" and covered with "eternal snow."

Zebulon Pike (1779–1813)
(continued)

Pike estimated that the base of this mountain was at least nineteen miles, or one day's march, away. According to his journal, Pike intended to put his party "in a defensible situation" and then to ascend this peak. His primary reason for doing so was that he believed its pinnacle would offer him the perfect vantage point from which to map the river branches and "unbounded prairies" that lay below.

But weather conditions forced Pike to reconsider this plan. Because his men were dressed in light overalls and had no socks, Pike concluded that they were "ill provided to endure the inclemency of the region." In his journal, Pike also expressed concern about the prospects of killing enough animals for food as they ascended the peak.

Instead, Pike and his party ascended the nearby but lower Cheyenne Mountain, a trip that was not without hardships. Thinking the climb would not take long, Pike and his men had left their baggage and provisions in a base camp. As a result, they slept on rocky ground, without blankets. They went for forty-eight hours without food, and they returned to camp to find their baggage safe but their provisions destroyed.

In 1813, Zebulon Pike was promoted to the rank of brigadier general. Later that same year, he was killed while commanding troops against York (which is now Toronto), Canada.

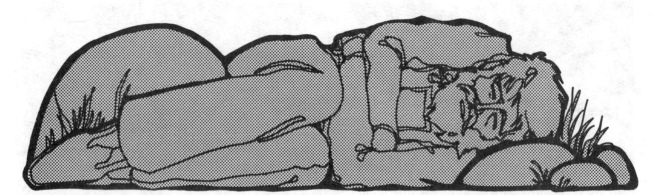

Activities

KN CO
1. On a map of Colorado, locate Pike's Peak. Then do some research to learn more about this mountain. How high is it? How does its height compare with that of other mountains in the continental United States? of other mountains in the world? In which range is it located? What towns is it near?

KN CO AP
2. Many geographic features have been named for the trailblazers who first laid eyes on them. For example, Beckwourth Pass was named for James Beckwourth, Carson Pass was named for Kit Carson, the Clark Fork was named for William Clark, and Pike's Peak was named for Zebulon Pike. Using an atlas and an encyclopedia or a biographical dictionary, make a list of ten additional geographic features that bear the names of their discoverers.

KN CO
3. The text above states that Toronto, Canada, was once called York. Do some research to learn about the history of this city. Who named it York? And how did its name come to be changed to Toronto?

KN CO
4. In his journal entries, Pike uses the words **commenced, confirmed, conjecture, defensible, encamped, endure, eternal, inclemency, inhabiting, pinnacle, ravine, summit, vegetation,** and **victuals**. Look up these words in a dictionary to learn what they mean and how they should be pronounced.

AP
5. Write an original journal entry in which you use at least six of the words listed in activity 4.

The Mountain Men

By 1750, many of the forests in the Old World had disappeared. For centuries, European villagers had been clearing the land for farms and using the wood for fuel and shelter. In many places, there were few trees among which fur-bearing animals could hunt and hide. As a result, parts of Europe were home to relatively few of these animals—certainly not enough to meet the growing demand for coats, hats, blankets, rugs, and other items of apparel and decoration.

At this same time in the New World, the forests stood thick and untouched. The Indians living in these woodlands gathered fallen branches but were little inclined to clear large areas. Before the white men came, these Indians hunted only the animals whose flesh they needed for food or whose hides they wanted for clothing or shelter but seldom killed for sport or profit.

The French explorers, who were among the first white men to see the interior of North America, recognized that much of the wealth of this new land lay in its abundant and untapped resources—its fertile land, its forests, and its fur-bearing animals. Instead of searching for gold, as the Spanish had done in Central and South America, these explorers traded for furs. From their homeland, they brought blankets, beads, bright-colored fabrics, bullets, guns, and metal tools to give to the Indians in exchange for animal pelts. The white men either traded these pelts farther east for supplies they needed or shipped them back to European cities, where they brought a handsome price.

These eager white traders built forts near Indian villages to facilitate trading and to protect their interests. As a result, many cities in what are now Canada and the United States actually began as fur-trading outposts, where white men came to get supplies and Indians came to exchange their pelts for the white man's goods. For example, St. Louis, Missouri, was an early center for the fur trade in the Midwest. These outposts, which were originally established to aid the fur trade, later became welcome way stations for settlers moving west.

At first, the Indians were the hunters and trappers, and the white men—who were often French or French Canadian—were merely the traders. But when white men realized that there was a fortune to be made in furs and that their share of it would be greater if they did not have to buy goods to trade with the Indians, some of them began to hunt and trap on their own.

These lone white trappers were often burly, bearded, buckskin-clad men whose appearance was as rugged as the country they roamed. They spent most of their time in the untamed wilderness, coming in contact with civilization only once or twice each year, when they came to a trading post to sell their pelts and to stock up on supplies. Among these hardy hunters and trappers were some who spent their time in and around both the Rocky Mountains and the Sierra Nevada and so earned the name **mountain men**.

The hunting and trapping experiences of the mountain men made them so familiar with western geography, woodcraft, and Indian lore that they were a natural choice to act as guides for pioneers headed west to California, Oregon, and Washington. Men like James Beckwourth, Jim Bridger, Joseph Walker, and Kit Carson all helped parties of settlers find their way safely over the majestic but treacherous mountains.

James Pierson Beckwourth (1798–*ca.* 1867) was a Virginia-born black hunter and adventurer who lived for a time with the Crow and other Indian tribes. Among other accomplishments, Beckwourth discovered (in 1851) the northern Sierra Nevada pass that bears his name and guided Ina Coolbrith and her family party to safety over it. **Jim Bridger** (1804–1881), who was also born in Virginia, is the first white man known to have visited the Great Salt Lake in what is now the state of Utah.

The Mountain Men
(continued)

Joseph Reddeford Walker (1798–1876) was born in Tennessee, became a frontiersman in Missouri, and was a member of Benjamin Bonneville's expedition to the Rocky Mountains in 1832. Walker's detachment of Bonneville's company made a westward crossing of the central Sierra in 1833 and were the first white men to do so. Much of their success can be attributed to Walker's careful planning. In preparation for the journey, he told each of his forty men to dry plenty of beef. He also had each man bring four horses, one to ride and three to carry supplies. And he asked Indians to recommend the best trails in the area. Although Walker and his men found crossing the desert and climbing the mountains difficult, they did not give up. Not one man turned back. And because of Walker's careful planning, not one man died. Later, Walker helped members of John Charles Frémont's second expedition to Oregon Territory find their way back east along the Spanish Trail and served as Frémont's principal guide on his third expedition. Both Walker Lake and Walker Pass (in the Tehachapi Mountains) are named for this remarkable trailblazer.

Christopher Carson (1809–1868), who is better known as Kit, was born in Kentucky but reared in Missouri. In 1826, he went to Santa Fe. Three years later, he joined a party of trappers who made their way from what is now New Mexico to California. Between 1831 and 1840, Carson became a leading mountain man, who was known for his Indian fighting and for his daring exploits. A chance meeting with John Charles Frémont during this time led to Carson's becoming a guide for Frémont's first two expeditions into Oregon Territory and to Carson's discovery, on the second expedition (1843–44), of the Sierra Nevada pass that bears his name.

Whatever the mountain men's reasons for venturing beyond the settled limits of a growing America, they deserve credit for blazing a trail for the missionaries, soldiers, and pioneers who followed. Though time has erased some of their names from the pages of history, their deeds have earned them an indelible place in United States lore as indispensible guides to the American West.

Activities

KN
CO

1. The white traders built forts near Indian villages to facilitate trading, and many cities in North America actually began as fur-trading outposts. Do some research to learn the names and locations of some of these outposts that became cities.

KN
CO
AP

2. Make a poster on which you show the animals that were hunted or trapped for their fur in North America during the eighteenth and nineteenth centuries.

KN
CO
AP
AN

3. Make an illustrated chart that shows in numbered steps each thing that happened to a pelt from the time it was taken from an animal in North America to the time it was sold as a finished garment in England or France.

AP
AN
SY

4. The fur trade seriously depleted the numbers of certain kinds of animals. Draw graphs that will enable you to compare the approximate numbers of beavers, foxes, rabbits, raccoons, seals, sea otters, and/or other fur-bearing mammals found in North America in 1650, 1750, 1850, and 1950 or some other similar series of dates.

KN
CO
AP

5. The bearded, burly, buckskin-clad mountain man is an ideal hero for a tall tale. Write a tall tale about a fictitious Beaver Bill or some other imagined and eccentric mountain man.

Name _____

Blazing the Trails

Settlers moving inland from the Atlantic Coast in search of more land blazed the trails that became America's first roads. In doing so, they followed footpaths used by herds of animals and by the Indians who hunted these animals.

The main obstacle to overland westward movement was the Appalachian Mountains. Actually, Appalachian Mountains is a general name for numerous mountain ranges in eastern North America. These mountains extend southwest from the St. Lawrence Valley in Canada to the Gulf Coast Plain in Alabama. They include the White Mountains, the Green Mountains, the Catskill Mountains, the Allegheny Mountains, the Blue Ridge Mountains, the Black Mountains, the Great Smoky Mountains, and other ranges.

The primary route across the northern section of the Appalachian Mountains was the **Mohawk Trail**, which ran along the Mohawk River from the Hudson River to the Great Lakes. Between 1763 and 1815, thousands of settlers followed this route; however, its use declined after the Erie Canal was completed in 1825.

The Appalachian Mountains have few natural passes, especially in the central section. For this reason, they presented a formidable barrier to pioneers who wanted to move inland from the Middle Atlantic States. The two main routes across this central section of the Appalachians were the Wilderness Road and the Cumberland or National Road.

The **Wilderness Road** was the trail blazed by Daniel Boone and his axmen in 1775. It stretched from the Holston River in Tennessee to the Kentucky River in Kentucky and passed through Cumberland Gap. Although this road was mountainous and rocky, within twenty-five years, 200,000 pioneers had used it on their way west.

Blazing the Trails
(continued)

Financed by the federal government, the **Cumberland Road**, or **National Road**, carried travelers from Cumberland, Maryland, through Pennsylvania, Ohio, and Indiana, to Vandalia, Illinois. This trail encouraged settlement west of the Ohio River.

The Mohawk Trail, the Wilderness Road, and the National Road all ran east and west. The **Natchez Trace** differed from these routes in that it ran north and south, from Nashville, Tennessee, to Natchez, Mississippi. It was a prominent commercial, military, and postal route during the 1800s.

By 1840, rivers and railroad tracks connected many of the important population centers in the East. Overland travel in this area by foot or wagon became less frequent. The old trails became less important and even fell into disuse.

At the same time, however, explorers, fur traders, missionaries, and mountain men were finding their way to Oregon Territory along the **Oregon Trail**. This route began in Independence, Missouri, and went through what are now the states of Kansas, Nebraska, Wyoming, and Idaho on its way to the Columbia River country. The Oregon Trail crossed the Great Plains and the Rocky Mountains. For two thousand miles, this longest overland trail tested the courage and endurance of pioneers who used it to reach the fertile valleys of the American Northwest. By the mid 1840s, more than ten thousand settlers had made the six-month journey, and the wheels of their wagons had carved ruts in the prairies so deep that they are still visible today.

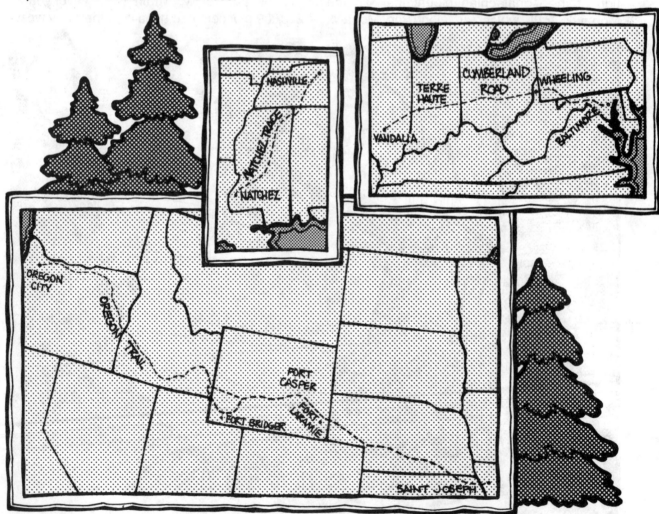

Name _____

Blazing the Trails
(continued)

Other trails were important to the settlement of the west. The **Santa Fe Trail** was a long commercial route from Independence, Missouri, to Santa Fe, New Mexico. Caravans of traders used this trail to carry manufactured goods west to trade for furs, mules, gold, and silver. As pioneers began to settle the Southwest, travel on this route increased. An extension of this route from Santa Fe west to Los Angeles, California, known as the **Spanish Trail**, carried both traders and settlers to the West Coast.

The **Chisholm Trail** was used by cowboys after the Civil War to drive vast herds of cattle north from Texas to railheads in Kansas for transport by train to the slaughterhouses and meat packing plants in the East. This trail was named for Jesse Chisholm, a half-breed Cherokee trader. In the spring of 1866, Chisholm drove a wagon loaded with buffalo hides north through Indian Territory (now the state of Oklahoma) to his trading post near Wichita, Kansas. The wheels of his heavy wagon cut deep ruts in the prairie floor, which was still soft from the seasonal rains. Under the scorching summer sun, these ruts hardened to mark a route that was followed for almost two decades. The westward extension of the railroads and the use of wire fences combined to put an end to traffic on the old Chisholm Trail, but it is still remembered in cowboy ballads and frontier lore.

Activities

KN
CO
1. One of the greatest needs of the pioneer settlers was roads over which they could transport their goods to markets in distant cities. Building roads in the wilderness was no easy task. Even after trees had been cut down and their stumps had been removed, the cleared area was little more than a wide path that was choked with dust in dry weather and became a muddy morass after each rain. Some of the first improved roads were **corduroy roads**, **macadam roads**, **plank roads**, and **turnpikes**, or **toll roads**. Define each of these types of road and explain the reason for its development.

KN
CO
AP
2. The era of the southwestern cattle drive was a colorful one. First, use at least three sources to gather information about this chapter in American history. Then, write an essay or short story about this period. Include detailed descriptions of a **trail drive** and of a typical **cow town**.

KN
CO
AP
AN
3. The Pony Express was begun on April 3, 1860, as a way of carrying mail swiftly from St. Joseph, Missouri, to Sacramento, California, along the Oregon Trail. The Butterfield Overland Mail made semiweekly stagecoach runs between St. Louis, Missouri, and both Los Angeles and San Francisco, California, via Arkansas; El Paso, Texas; and Tucson and Yuma, Arizona. Do some research to learn more about the fierce rivalry that existed for a time between these two mail services, the routes they used, and the inventions and developments that eventually made both of them obsolete.

AN
SY
EV
4. Between May 1804 and September 1806, the Lewis and Clark expedition spent more than 2½ years traveling over 8,000 miles, from St. Louis, Missouri, to Astoria, Washington, on foot, by boat, and on horseback. During the 1840s, pioneer wagon trains took 6 months to go 2,000 miles, from Independence, Missouri, to Oregon Territory along the Oregon Trail. In 1858, a Butterfield stagecoach made its first 2,800-mile run from St. Louis, Missouri, to San Francisco, California, in 24 days, 18 hours, and 26 minutes. In 1860, Pony Express riders made the run from St. Joseph, Missouri, to Sacramento, California, along the Oregon Trail in 10 days. First, make a chart or table on which you compare these times and distances. Then, add others you encounter in your reading about this period. Finally, create a time line showing some of the technical developments and improvements that eventually cut the time required to go from Missouri to California from one year or more to a few hours. In making your time line, consider both the means by which people made this journey and the surfaces over which they traveled.

"Oregon or Bust"

During the 1830s, Oregon Territory was a vast wilderness made up of what are now the states of Washington, Oregon, and Idaho, and parts of Wyoming and Montana. It was inhabited primarily by Indians. The only white men who lived in this area were British and American fur trappers and traders. In fact, the first wagon train of pioneers to travel the Oregon Trail and reach Columbia River country, which was led by Elijah White, did not arrive until 1842.

But six years earlier, in 1836, a small party of Presbyterian missionaries, intent upon working among the Indians, left Missouri and drove their wagons west on the Oregon Trail as far as Fort Boise in what is now Idaho. These missionaries are credited with opening that part of the Oregon Trail for wagon travel. In this party of trailblazers were Dr. Marcus Whitman, his wife Narcissa, the Reverend Henry Spalding, and his wife Eliza. Their treacherous journey west took from May until September. At its end, Narcissa Whitman and Eliza Spalding became the first white women to cross the Continental Divide and settle west of the Rocky Mountains.

Marcus Whitman was born in Rushville, New York, in 1802, and graduated from that state's Fairfield Medical School in 1832. Three years later, he left a country medical practice to become a missionary. Accompanied by the Reverend Samual Parker, Whitman rode west to take a first-hand look at Oregon Territory and to see what the physical and spiritual needs of the Indians might be. On this preliminary fact-finding journey, the two men traveled with the caravan of the American Fur Company on the Oregon Trail.

Parker kept a journal of their travels. About the American Fur Company he wrote, "[They] have between two and three hundred men constantly in and about the mountains, engaged in trading, hunting and trapping. These all assemble at rendezvous upon the arrival of the caravan, bring in their furs, and take new supplies for the coming year, of clothing, ammunition, and goods for trade with the Indians. But few of these men ever return to their country and friends. Most of them are constantly in debt to the company, and are unwilling to return without a fortune; and year after year passes away, while they are hoping in vain for better success."

Parker also wrote about Whitman's performing a surgical operation in which he "extracted an iron arrow, three inches long, from the back of Capt. Bridger, which was received in a skirmish, three years before, with the Blackfeet Indians." Commented Parker, "It was a difficult operation, because the arrow was hooked at the point by striking a large bone, and a cartilaginous substance had grown around it. The Doctor pursued the operation with great self-possession and perseverance; and his patient manifested equal firmness. The Indians looked on meanwhile, with countenances indicating wonder, and in their own peculiar manner expressed great astonishment when it was extracted."

Name _____

"Oregon or Bust"
(continued)

When Whitman returned to the East, he married Narcissa Prentiss. Born in Prattsburg, New York, she had grown up on a farm and had become a teacher. Shortly after her marriage to Whitman in 1836, the two of them and the Spaldings were sent by the joint Presbyterian-Congregationalist Board of Missions to minister to the Indians of the Pacific Northwest. The Spaldings established a mission at Lapwai, near the present Lewiston, Idaho. The Whitmans founded a mission at Waiilatpu, near what is now Walla Walla, Washington.

In 1842, Marcus Whitman rode east to clear up a misunderstanding with the mission board, gain additional support for his missionary effort, and encourage Americans to emigrate to Oregon. Whitman returned with the "great emigration" of 1843, in which more than nine hundred settlers, with the words "Oregon or Bust" painted on their wagons and with one thousand head of stock in tow, followed the Oregon Trail to Oregon Territory. By that year, the Whitman mission consisted of several buildings and served as a welcome way station for trail-weary travelers.

For a time, everything went well for the Whitmans in Oregon Territory. Marcus preached the Gospel and treated the sick. Narcissa managed the household and taught school. But in 1847, the new settlers brought with them a measles epidemic. The Whitmans were able to save most of the white children, but their medicine was powerless to help the Indian children, who had never been exposed to the disease and had no natural resistance. Many of them died.

On November 29, 1847, a band of Cayuse Indians, who probably believed that their children had been poisoned by the white man's medicine, attacked the mission. They killed Whitman, his wife, and twelve other persons, and burned all of the mission buildings. When news of this tragic massacre reached Washington, it hastened the passage of a bill officially declaring Oregon a United States territory.

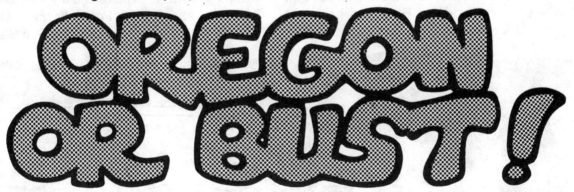

Activities

KN CO
1. A measles epidemic is suspected of triggering the tragic massacre in which the Whitmans were killed. Do some research to learn about measles. What kind of disease is it? What are its symptoms? How is it spread? How was it treated then? How is it treated today? What part do antibodies play in its prevention? Why would white children who apparently had not had the disease have more resistance to it than Indian children who had never been exposed to it?

CO AP AN
2. Narcissa Whitman and Eliza Spalding were the first white women to cross the Continental Divide and travel overland to settle west of the Rocky Mountains. Why was it unusual for two women to be among those traveling westward at that time? In what ways did Narcissa Whitman and Eliza Spalding blaze a trail for other women who made the same difficult journey after them?

AN SY
3. Compare the Whitmans' journey westward with that of Lewis and Clark. In what ways were these journeys similar? In what ways were they different? Consider the routes these travelers followed, the means by which they traveled, and the purposes of their journeys.

The Pathfinder of the West

When John Charles Frémont died in 1890 at the age of seventy-seven, he had a long list of accomplishments to his credit. For example, he had served in both the Army and the Navy. He had been instrumental in winning California for the United States and had been elected as one of the first two U.S. senators from that state. He had commanded the Union Army in the West for a time and had served as territorial governor of Arizona from 1878 to 1883. And he had been the first candidate nominated for the office of president of the United States by the new Republican Party. Yet, none of these achievements won for him as much fame as his mapping expeditions in the West. Because of these efforts, he earned lasting recognition as the "Pathfinder of the West."

John Charles Frémont was born in Savannah, Georgia, in 1813. As a youth, he had a great interest in both botany and mathematics. He entered Charleston College but, because of his restless spirit, was forced to leave that campus before earning his degree. For a time, he taught math to U.S. naval cadets. Then, he became an officer in the Topographical Corps of the U.S. Army. In this capacity, he accompanied Joseph Nicolas Nicollet on a surveying expedition between the upper Mississippi and the Missouri rivers. Nicollet, a French scientist, proved to be an excellent teacher. From him Frémont learned how to use stars and star charts to determine his precise location and how to explore lands systematically, draw maps accurately, and keep records carefully.

Upon Frémont's return to the East, he eloped with a young woman named Jessie Benton, the daughter of Thomas Hart Benton, a senator from Missouri. At first upset by the match, Benton eventually became reconciled to it and even helped his son-in-law secure command of an expedition to explore the Des Moines River in 1841. Subsequently, under congressional authority, Frémont led three expeditions into Oregon Territory between 1842 and 1845.

On the first expedition in 1842, Frémont's assignment was to explore and map the Oregon Trail as far as the South Pass. His guide for this trip was the famous mountain man, Kit Carson.

The Pathfinder of the West
(continued)

In the following year, Frémont and a party of forty men, including Kit Carson, were ordered into Oregon Territory once again to explore and map the remainder of the Oregon Trail. Frémont's instructions were to explore the area immediately south of the Columbia River, between the Rocky Mountains and the Pacific Ocean; but when he had completed this assignment, the adventurer could not resist the siren call of what he termed the "Great Basin." Long fascinated by these desert-like plains that extend from parts of Utah and most of Nevada into southeastern California, Frémont decided to survey this region also. Even as winter approached, Frémont led his men south through Oregon into Nevada and then west toward the base of the Sierra Nevada, the majestic gateway to what was then Mexican California.

Winter reached the mountains ahead of the hapless expedition. Snow was twenty feet deep in some places, and it was nearly impossible to get horses and supplies over the steep, rugged peaks. Frémont's Indian guides abandoned him, and both his men and his animals grew weak and hungry.

Carson had been in these mountains before but never under such conditions. He did not know an easy way across, but he did know that party members could ill afford to exhaust their waning energy by wandering aimlessly in search of one. Instead, he and Frémont fashioned crude snowshoes for themselves and a small group of men. Together, they searched for and found the pass that brought them all safely out of the mountains and into the Sacramento Valley. Today, this pass still bears Carson's name.

Frémont's expedition moved south through California; and, with the help of Joseph Walker, a frontiersman and trailblazer, returned home over the Spanish Trail. Once home, Frémont described his adventures in a Senate-sponsored document called the *Report of the Exploring Expedition to Oregon and North California*, which was published in 1845. Despite its tedious accounting of the latitudes and longitudes and of the flora and fauna, this document received a warm reception from the public. It stimulated the belief in manifest destiny, encouraged settlement of the West, and anticipated a war with Mexico over ownership of California.

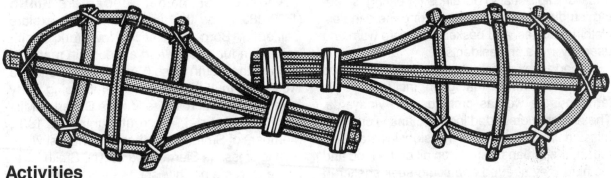

Activities

KN CO 1. Jessie Benton's father was not the only Thomas Hart Benton to earn a place in history. Do some research to learn about another well-known man with the same name. Where was he born? What did he do? In what way was he related to Jessie's father?

CO AP 2. In 1856, John Charles Frémont was nominated by the new Republican Party as its first candidate for the office of president of the United States. Write a speech Frémont might have used during his unsuccessful campaign against Democrat James Buchanan. In this speech, describe the accomplishments that would have qualified Frémont for the presidency and include the campaign slogan he actually used or create one you think would be appropriate.

AN 3. Make a list of the geographic features that were named for or by Kit Carson and John Charles Frémont. Include lakes, mountains, passes, and rivers, as well as cities and towns. Document the origin of each name through your reading, and pinpoint each location on a United States map.

The Bear Flag Republic

By 1700, because of a series of explorations and conquests, Spain ruled much of South America, Central America, and Mexico. At that time, what is now Mexico was called New Spain.

In 1769, the ruler of New Spain sent a group of people north to live in California. In this group were soldiers, Indians from New Spain, and two Franciscan friars. **Friars** were Catholic priests who traveled and taught people about their religion. They were Catholic missionaries who wanted to Christianize the Indians of California just as the Whitmans were Presbyterian missionaries who wanted to Christianize the Indians of Oregon Territory. One of these friars was Father Junípero Serra.

Father Serra was an intensely dedicated man who pursued his missionary work with uncommon zeal. Between 1769 and 1782, he established the first nine missions in a chain that would eventually stretch from San Diego to Sonoma and number twenty-one. Placed approximately one day's walk apart, these missions were more than mere churches. They were actually tiny but self-sufficient towns built within the safety of thick walls. They included not only buildings for prayer and worship but also buildings for eating, sleeping, studying, storing, and making the candles, clothing, dishes, and baskets that were worn and used by mission residents.

Managed by friars, the missions controlled great landholdings that often included fertile farmlands as well as orchards and vineyards. These friars persuaded local Indians to cultivate mission lands and herd mission livestock. In return, the Indians were given all of the food and clothing they needed and could seek shelter in mission buildings and protection within mission walls.

For a long time, Americans knew little about California. They were separated from it by an unexplored continent. Some contact was made by ship, but the idea of developing an overland route was abandoned in the late 1700s because of repeated Indian massacres.

A trailblazer named **Jedediah Smith** (1799–1831) was the first American to explore California. Born in 1799 in New York, Smith became a fur trapper and a mountain man. He opened the South Pass (Wyoming) route to the West and, in 1826, led a beaver-trapping party from Salt Lake across the Mojave Desert to Mission San Gabriel. En route home in 1827, members of Smith's party became the first white men to cross the Sierra Nevada. The Smith River in the extreme northwest corner of California is named for the man who first blazed a trail to this state.

The Bear Flag Republic
(continued)

During the early part of the nineteenth century, there was renewed interest in finding an overland route to the Pacific. Between 1804 and 1806, Lewis and Clark found one route; but in the 1840s, John Charles Frémont led mapping expeditions in search of another. Frémont's success was instrumental in convincing Americans to move to California.

By this time, Mexico had gained its independence from Spain, and California had become a Mexican possession. As more and more Americans moved to California, they became less and less willing to submit to foreign rule. In 1846, while the United States was at war with Mexico over the boundary between Texas and that country, a band of Californians joined the revolt. Led by Ezekiel Merritt—who was described by some of his contemporaries as a "coarse-grained, unprincipled, quarrelsome fellow"—they seized a Mexican fort at Sonoma. Atop the fort they unfurled a homemade flag bearing a star, a grizzly bear, and the words "California Republic." This event became known as the "Bear Flag Revolt," and California was called the "Bear Flag Republic." When the Mexican War ended on February 2, 1848, with the signing of the Treaty of Guadalupe Hidalgo, the Bear Flag Republic officially became a United States territory.

Gold! Mere mention of that word had inspired New World exploration for centuries. Spanish conquistadores searched for gold in South America, Mexico, and Florida. But their searches were far from James Marshall's mind as he supervised the deepening of the channel at John Augustus Sutter's new sawmill on the South Fork of the American River near its junction with the Sacramento. On January 24, 1848, Marshall suddenly stopped the workers, bent down, and searched through the water. The shiny rocks he picked up changed the West forever. They were gold.

In these words, Sutter described the day on which Marshall told him of the discovery: "I was sitting one afternoon just after my siesta, engaged, by-the-bye, in writing a letter to a relation of mine at Lucern [Switzerland], when I was interrupted by Mr. Marshall, a gentleman with whom I had frequent business transactions—bursting into the room. From the unusual agitation in his manner I imagined that something serious had occurred, and, . . . I at once glanced to see if my rifle was in its proper place."

But Sutter's rifle was useless in this emergency. Word of Marshall's discovery traveled fast. When it reached the East, men set out for California to stake their own claims. By 1849, a large-scale gold rush had begun. Nearly 100,000 eager prospectors swelled the population of California. By 1850, this territory had enough people to be admitted to the Union as the thirty-first state.

Activities

KN CO AP
1. California's history is long and colorful. Make an illustrated time line covering some of the important dates and events that make up this history.

KN CO AP AN SY
2. Before the arrival of the Spaniards in the eighteenth century, many Indian tribes had inhabited parts of California for at least eleven thousand years. First, do some research to learn about these Indians. Then, make a map showing where some of the different tribes lived. Finally, write an in-depth report on one of the tribes in which you describe this group's life-style and explain the ways in which it differed from those of the Woodland and Plains Indians.

AN SY
3. Large ranchos were common during the Mexican occupation of California. Compare the ranchos of Mexican California with the plantations of the South before the Civil War. In what ways were they similar? In what ways were they different?

Correlated Activities

KN
CO
AP

Make a series of drawings depicting the various means of transportation used by pioneers. Color and label each drawing. As part of your label, tell when each means of transportation was used and by whom.

KN
CO
AP
SY

Make a replica of the flag that mountain man and trapper Ezekiel Merritt and his frontiersmen unfurled at the captured Mexican headquarters in California. Write a one-act play in which the capture of this fort is reenacted. Stage this play with the help of some of your classmates. Use the flag as your central prop.

KN
CO
AP
SY

To pass the time on long trail drives and to keep the cattle pacified, cowboys often sang songs. These ballads told stories about long, lonely days in the saddle, disquieting night sounds, and restless, milling herds. First, find copies of some trail songs and read the lyrics. Then, retell one of these songs in your own words. Finally, for another song, write an additional verse about a real or imagined travel adventure.

KN
CO
AP

Cowboys developed a "language" that was peculiar to their own colorful way of life. The following terms were a part of this language:

bronco	necktie social
buckaroo	nester
chuck wagon	paint
cinch	remuda
cowpoke	road agent
cowpuncher	roundup
dogie	rustler
greenhorn	shindig
hackamore	stetson
lariat	tenderfoot
lasso	vaquero
maverick	waddy
mustang	wrangler

Use these terms to create an illustrated **Cowboy Dictionary**. Print each word on a separate sheet of paper. Beside the term, show in parentheses how it should be pronounced. Below the term, write its definition or description. Then, write a sentence in which you use the term. Finally, on the bottom half of the sheet of paper, draw and label a picture that will help you remember what the term means. Punch three holes down the left-hand side of each one of these sheets, and tie them together with yarn or place them in a three-ring binder. Add a new page to your dictionary each time you encounter another cowboy term.

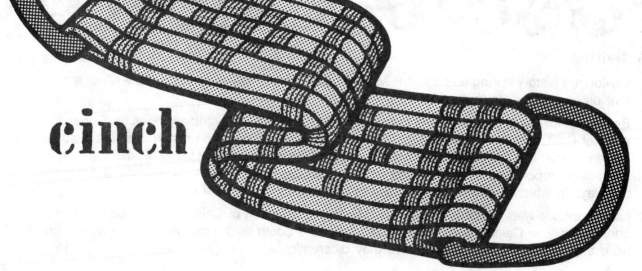

cinch

Correlated Activities
(continued)

KN CO AP History sometimes gives the impression that all of the frontiers have been tamed and that all of the trails have been blazed. Nothing could be further from the truth. For those who know where to look, there are still trails to blaze and frontiers to explore. The people listed below have blazed trails to little-known frontiers. Do some research to learn what special frontier interested each one of these trailblazers and what he or she accomplished by exploring it.

Ansel Adams	Thor Heyerdahl
Neil Armstrong	Sir Edmund Hillary
Admiral Richard Byrd	John Muir
Jacques Cousteau	Auguste Piccard
Charles Darwin	Dick Rutan
Robin Lee Graham	Jeana Yeager

Read the newspapers and watch the news to see what trails are being blazed today. Make modern-day trailblazers the subject of a special bulletin board or classroom current events display.

KN CO AP AN SY EV Biosphere II is a sealed-off, self-contained ecological system that will be used by eight pioneers to "blaze the trail for outer space." Under construction in Arizona in the Santa Catalina Mountains on the edge of the Sonora Desert, this sprawling 2.25-acre steel-and-glass structure will enclose five million cubic feet and will contain seven different ecological zones, including a tropical rain forest, an ocean, a marshland, a savannah, and a desert when finished. Its volunteer residents—who are being called "Biospherians"—will enter this special environment in December 1989 and lock the door behind them. For the next two years, they will receive only sunlight and electronic communication from the outside. They will have to grow their own food and use their resources wisely so that their needs are met and nothing is wasted. Do some research to learn more about Biosphere II. Compare the participants in this experiment with the trailblazers about whom you have read. In what ways are they similar? In what ways are they different? Compare life in Biosphere II with prolonged travel through space. In what ways might these two adventures be similar? In what ways might they be different? Is the earth a closed ecological system? Why or why not? What valuable lessons about life on earth can we learn from the pioneer residents of Biosphere II?

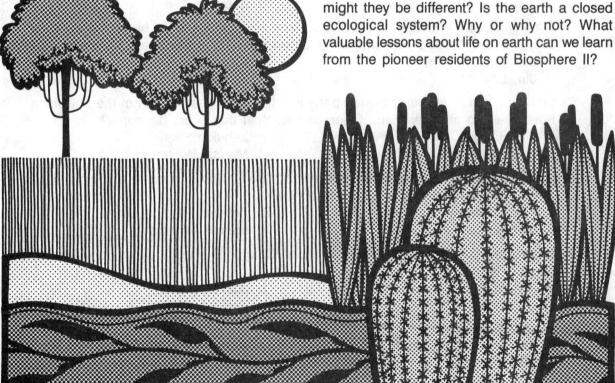

Name _____

Posttest

Circle the letter beside the best answer or the most appropriate response.

1. Which trailblazer led pioneer families through the Cumberland Gap into Kentucky?
   a. James Beckwourth
   b. Daniel Boone
   c. Kit Carson
   d. George Rogers Clark

2. Which Revolutionary frontier leader used his own money to hire the small band of soldiers that captured three British forts to protect the rights of American colonists to the Ohio River Valley?
   a. George Rogers Clark
   b. William Clark
   c. Toussaint Charbonneau
   d. John Charles Frémont

3. The main reason the United States wanted the Louisiana Territory was to
   a. give pioneer farmers more land.
   b. give Lewis and Clark something to explore.
   c. protect shipping and trade routes.
   d. increase United States landholdings.

4. Which trailblazers found a route across the American continent from St. Louis, Missouri, to the Pacific Ocean?
   a. James Beckwourth and Jim Bridger
   b. Kit Carson and John Charles Frémont
   c. Meriwether Lewis and George Rogers Clark
   d. Meriwether Lewis and William Clark

5. Which trailblazer is the first white man known to have visited the Great Salt Lake?
   a. James Beckwourth
   b. Jim Bridger
   c. John Charles Fremont
   d. Zebulon Pike

6. Which mountain man carried Ina Coolbrith on his saddle and led her family to safety over a Sierra Nevada pass that he discovered and that now bears his name?
   a. James Beckwourth
   b. Jim Bridger
   c. Kit Carson
   d. James Marshall

7. Which trailblazer led an exploring party into the southwestern part of the Louisiana Purchase and discovered the Colorado mountain that bears his name?
   a. Jim Bridger
   b. Kit Carson
   c. Zebulon Pike
   d. Marcus Whitman

8. Which trailblazer was murdered by Cayuse Indians after a measles epidemic killed many Indian children in Oregon Territory?
   a. James Beckwourth
   b. James Marshall
   c. Zebulon Pike
   d. Marcus Whitman

9. Which trailblazer acted as a guide on John Charles Frémont's expeditions into the Oregon Territory?
   a. Jim Bridger
   b. Kit Carson
   c. Joseph Nicollet
   d. Zebulon Pike

10. James Marshall
    a. fought at the Alamo in Texas.
    b. discovered gold in California.
    c. explored the Northwest Territory.
    d. discovered a mountain pass.

Answer Key

Pretest, Page 80		Posttest, Page 110	
1. c	6. b	1. b	6. a
2. a	7. a	2. a	7. c
3. c	8. b	3. c	8. d
4. a	9. a	4. d	9. b
5. c	10. d	5. b	10. b

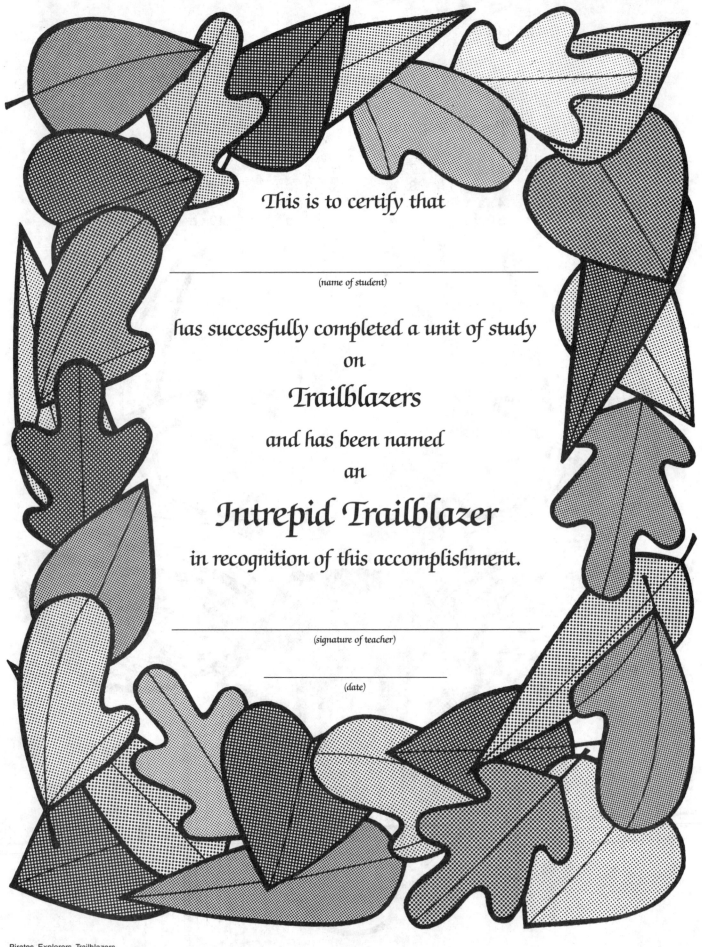

This is to certify that

_____
(name of student)

has successfully completed a unit of study
on
Trailblazers
and has been named
an

Intrepid Trailblazer

in recognition of this accomplishment.

_____
(signature of teacher)

_____
(date)